What's Space Got To Do With It?

10 Life Lessons For Personal Growth

Shelli Brunswick

SB Global, LLC.

ISBN-13: 979-8-9916950-0-8

Cover design by: Keelan Bailey

Printed in the United States of America

DEDICATION

To my mother, whose strength, resilience, and kindness have been my guiding light. Your unwavering support and belief in me have fueled my dreams and taught me the power of perseverance. To my husband, my greatest supporter, your constant encouragement and faith in my abilities inspire me to pursue my passions fearlessly. You motivate me to reach for the stars and follow my heart. This book is dedicated to you both with endless gratitude for your daily love and inspiration.

DEDICATION

ACKNOWLEDGEMENTS

Writing *What's Space Got To Do With It: 10 Life Lessons for Personal Growth* has been a deeply personal and transformative journey. This book reflects my experiences and the wisdom and insights of those who have guided, inspired, and supported me. I offer my heartfelt gratitude to everyone who has been part of this journey.

Special Thanks

First, I want to thank *Dr. Timothy Mottet*, former President of Colorado State University-Pueblo (CSU-P), whose invitation for me to deliver the 2022 spring commencement address sparked the genesis of this book. Your encouragement to share my authentic journey and your belief in the power of storytelling laid the foundation for its creation.

None of this would have been possible without the unwavering support of my family. I want to thank my *Aunt Barb* and *Uncle Randy* for their constant love and encouragement. You have been pillars of strength throughout this journey, and your belief in me has fueled my drive.

I am deeply grateful to the global thought leaders who contributed their time, wisdom, and insights to this book. Their interviews provided a rich tapestry of perspectives that shaped the lessons and insights shared here. Their short biographies are included at the end of this book.

Creative and Strategic Contributions

Keelan Bailey, a talented artist I've known through the higher education world, your creativity not only brought the cover of this book to life but also shaped the *What's Space Got To Do With It?* and the SB Global LLC logos and so much more. I am immensely grateful for your vision, artistry, and ongoing support.

Ami Patel, your leadership, business acumen, and friendship have been a constant source of strength. You created my website and were a trusted sounding board for ideas throughout this journey. Our collaboration through the WomenTech Network and various projects has been incredibly enriching, and I am deeply grateful for your unwavering support.

Rachael Rhine Milliard, whom I met through the *Behavioral International Economic Development* (BIED) *Society* while writing an article on Authentic Leadership with Peter Hu, graciously took on editing this book. Her editorial expertise and attention to detail were invaluable in shaping the final product. I'm deeply grateful for her dedication and commitment to bringing this project to completion.

Acknowledgment of Chapter Reviewers

I am deeply grateful to the incredible individuals who took the time to review chapters of this book, offering valuable feedback and insights that helped shape the final product.

- *Tom Bugnitz*, thank you for inviting me to join the Manufacturer's Edge Board of Directors, which significantly expanded my growth. Your mentorship has been instrumental in my understanding of leadership and innovation.
- *Diane Dimeff*, your mentorship in developing the space commerce program at Space Foundation has been a cornerstone of my journey. Your leadership fueled my passion for the global space ecosystem.
- *Yira Muse*, your strategic insights and leadership in policy have been a constant source of inspiration since our time as US Air Force legislative liaisons.
- *Wayne Anderson*, serving with you on the Manufacturer's Edge board has been a privilege. Your leadership contributed greatly to the development of this book.
- *Dr. Jack Gregg*, your guidance in shaping the new

space economy has deeply influenced my work. I remain inspired by your book *The Cosmos Economy*.

• *Dr. Vanessa Farsadaki*, your dedication to advancing space medicine and international partnerships is truly inspiring.

• *Jen Blank*, your role as a leader in the G100 and the broader space ecosystem is inspiring.

• *Gabriella Goddard*, your mentorship and support have been pivotal to the success of this series.

To everyone who has been a part of this journey, thank you. Your support, guidance, and friendship have made this book—and the series—possible.

CONTENTS

WHAT'S SPACE GOT TO DO WITH IT? A SERIES

What's Space Got to Do With It? is a focused research project designed to capture the collective wisdom of decades of multinational space leadership and share it with aspiring leaders around the world. My research draws lessons from space innovation and leadership practitioners. My goal for this series is to embolden both current and future leaders to dream big, act boldly, and achieve greatness. My hope is to elevate the readers' perspectives and encourage them to reach for the stars, metaphorically and literally.

In the evolving landscape of our professional and personal lives, the principles that guide us are as universal as the cosmic laws governing the universe. These principles are not just abstract ideas but practical tools that help us navigate the complexities of leadership, innovation, and personal growth. Drawing from over 35 years of experience in the aerospace and space industries and enriched by the wisdom of over 200 global thought leaders, this series of books is designed to offer insights that eclipse conventional boundaries. Whether you work in technology, education, finance, or another field, the lessons shared here are meant to inspire you, the reader, to seize opportunities, overcome challenges, and achieve meaningful success.

The space industry plays a crucial role in shaping the lessons of this book series because it drives, and will continue to drive, global economic growth and innovation for the rest of this century and beyond. The insights gained from the space industry's rapid advancements serve as a powerful model for leadership, resilience, and vision—qualities that are essential not only in space but in every field.

As more colleges and universities offer courses and programs in space business management and leadership, these books will be an essential read for emerging and established leaders, regardless of their background, region, or career stage.

Mission and Vision

My mission is to bridge the gap between space innovation and everyday leadership. By distilling the key lessons learned from the space industry, each book in the *What's Space Got to Do With It?* series will provide practical guidance for navigating the complexities of leadership and personal growth in any context. My vision is to make these insights accessible and applicable across a wide range of industries and careers, empowering the reader to unlock their full potential and thrive in an ever-changing world.

Overview of the First Book

As the first book in this series, *10 Life Lessons for Personal Growth* lays the foundation for your leadership journey. This book focuses on core principles that have shaped my career, along with lessons learned from the global thought leaders I've had the privilege of working with. These lessons will inspire you to elevate your leadership, embrace opportunities, and overcome challenges with resilience and confidence. It serves as a guide for personal and professional growth, offering key takeaways you can immediately apply to your life.

The Roadmap for Your Transformational Journey

This book is meticulously crafted to take you on a transformative journey, offering both inspiration and practical advice. Each chapter begins with a comprehensive overview of key leadership and personal development concepts, providing a framework for the following lessons.

Personal Reflections

To bring these concepts to life, I share Personal Reflections—intimate stories and insights from my journey. These reflections offer a unique insider's perspective on success, challenges, and lessons that have shaped my path. Through these stories, I aim to connect with you on a personal level, demonstrating how these principles have influenced my career and how they can shape yours as well.

Leadership Stories

In addition to my personal reflections, each chapter features insights and stories from three Global Thought Leader interviews. These visionaries have significantly contributed to their respective fields and offer diverse perspectives that can be applied to your own challenges and goals. Their stories offer practical examples of how the principles discussed in each chapter can be applied across various industries and contexts. For those interested in learning more about these leaders, their short biographies are included at the end of the book.

Insights into Action

To help these lessons translate into tangible results, each chapter concludes with a section called Transforming Insights into Action. This section offers clear steps for integrating these principles into daily routines and long-term strategies.

References

Finally, every chapter concludes with a References section, providing original sources of ideas, insights, and additional resources. This ensures you can explore the content further and dive deeper into the topics that resonate most with you.

This comprehensive structure—blending theoretical insights with practical applications, personal stories, and expert advice—is designed to inspire and empower you to make meaningful progress in your career and personal life. By following the guidance in each chapter, you can build a foundation for success that is resilient and adaptable to the challenges of a rapidly changing world.

A Note of Clarification

The purpose of this book is to provide encouragement, information, and inspiration. It is intended for educational and informational purposes only. While every effort has been made to ensure accuracy, the author and publisher acknowledge that individual success depends on various personal factors and circumstances. Therefore, this book cannot guarantee specific outcomes, and I assume no responsibility for any actions or decisions based on this book's content. Readers are encouraged to conduct further research and apply their own judgment.

CHAPTER ONE SEIZING COSMIC OPPORTUNITIES: UNLEASHING YOUR POTENTIAL BY TAKING ADVANTAGE OF EVERY OPPORTUNITY

"In the cosmos of our careers, opportunities are like rare celestial events—fleeting yet transformative. To capture them, we must be perpetually prepared, always poised with the telescope of our skills and knowledge aimed at the horizons of possibility."

Shelli Brunswick

Opportunities are not just stepping stones but the transformative catalysts that guide our career paths, drive personal growth, and unlock hidden potential. Whether in technology, space, education, or any other field, recognizing and seizing these opportunities requires a blend of awareness, preparation, and courage. Through my experiences and interviews with global thought leaders, I've learned that the power of embracing opportunities lies in the moment of action and the mindset that allows us to see and capture them. These narratives offer practical advice on identifying opportunities, preparing to seize them, and using them as rocket fuel for career advancement and personal growth.

Opportunities are often wrapped in a paradox. They are, by their very nature, disruptive. They challenge established routines, demand time and energy, and push us beyond our comfort zones. This inherent disruption can trigger resistance, leading to postponed or avoided action. But it's crucial to remember that some of the most transformative moments in life arise from these very disruptions. Imagine if Marie Curie, faced with the inconvenience of late-night lab work, had chosen the comfort of sleep instead. Or if Steve Jobs had opted for the conventional path rather than dropping out of college and embracing the uncertainty that led to groundbreaking innovations. The greatest advancements often come from embracing the disruptive nature of opportunity. This is where courage and readiness to face challenges come into play.

As Richard Branson wisely said, "If someone offers you an amazing opportunity and you're not sure you can do it, say yes —then learn how to do it later." Embracing disruption can lead to innovation, growth, and remarkable achievement. The key is to recognize that these challenging moments are often the gateways to our most significant successes.

But how do we recognize these opportunities? Not all of them announce themselves with fanfare. Often, they appear as mundane tasks or unexpected challenges. The importance of awareness cannot be overstated. It's about staying informed, understanding your environment, and recognizing potential in every situation. By keeping an eye on emerging trends, market shifts, and developments in your field, you can anticipate change and position yourself to take advantage of new opportunities. Embracing a proactive approach allows you to navigate your career with foresight and agility, and stay ahead in a rapidly evolving landscape.

Awareness and mindfulness also help you see potential in everyday moments. When viewed through the lens of opportunity, the seemingly insignificant becomes a springboard for advancement. Adopting this mindset transforms routine activities into meaningful experiences, contributing to professional and personal growth.

By welcoming disruption and maintaining awareness, you

can unlock your potential and significantly impact your field. The future belongs to those willing to step outside their comfort zones, seize opportunities, and contribute to a brighter, more innovative world for themselves and others. As you journey through these insights, let them inspire you to view every challenge as a potential opportunity.

Personal Reflections

My journey into the space industry began when I enlisted in the United States Air Force (USAF) right out of high school. I didn't have money to go to college, and I wasn't sure what I wanted to study if I did. I wanted to see the world, and the Air Force presented a perfect opportunity to earn college money, learn a profession, and see the world.

I was stationed in Turkey, Germany, and at the United States Air Force Academy in Colorado Springs during my service. These assignments immersed me in different cultures and taught me about people and customs outside the bubble I had grown up in. As a personnel and human resources specialist, I learned about customer service, promotions, training, and benefits, which gave me a skill set and a career path.

One of the most significant opportunities I seized was the chance to further my education. While working during the day, I used the Tuition Assistance Program to complete my bachelor's and master's degrees by attending classes at night. This pivotal step allowed me to apply and be accepted as an officer in the USAF, eventually leading to my career in the space industry.

My journey as an officer in the Air Force opened many doors for me, particularly in the space industry. I was chosen to be a Space Program Manager, marking the beginning of my 25-year career in this fascinating field. I took on challenging projects, volunteered for difficult tasks, and continuously sought ways to improve my leadership skills and knowledge as a space professional. These experiences taught me the importance of seizing every opportunity, no matter how daunting it might seem.

Insights From Global Thought Leaders

"In the cosmos of career and life, the gravity of opportunity pulls those who are prepared. Never stop learning; your next giant leap may require knowledge you gather today."

H.E. Dr. Rosalía Arteaga.

H.E. Dr. Rosalía Arteaga, a distinguished figure in education, politics, and cultural advocacy, serves as the CEO of the FIDAL Foundation and President of UNIR-Ecuador. She holds the remarkable distinction of being the first female President of Ecuador, after being elected to Vice President by popular vote. Dr. Arteaga's journey is marked by resilience, an unyielding commitment to learning, and a dedication to empowering the next generation. Her career spans various sectors, demonstrating her ability to adapt her skills to diverse scenarios.

Her journey began with a deep passion for education. At just 17, Dr. Arteaga was asked to become a teacher—which initially astonished her due to her young age. Teaching had always seemed reserved for older, more experienced individuals. However, her intellectual maturity and dedication to learning made her an ideal candidate. Accepting this challenge, she quickly discovered a deep love for teaching, and that became a foundational part of her lifelong commitment to education. This early start paved the way for a career dedicated to inspiring others. Dr. Arteaga spent over 20 years as a high school teacher while pursuing her writing and journalism interests. Teaching was more than a profession for her—it was a mission that instilled her belief in the power of knowledge and inspired her desire to help others reach their fullest potential.

Dr. Arteaga's career took a significant turn when she was invited to serve as Undersecretary of Culture. That role was followed by her appointment as Minister of Education, Culture, and Sports. Her proactive approach in these roles involved proposing new curricula and visiting schools to understand and address their needs directly. Her educational leadership was transformative, gaining support from authorities and teachers.

Her role in public service reached a historic milestone when she briefly assumed the presidency of Ecuador in 1997, becoming the first woman to hold this esteemed office. However, her tenure was abruptly cut short due to a coup involving military forces and the Ecuadorian Congress. Despite the brevity of her presidency, Dr. Arteaga's resilience during this turbulent time highlighted her strength and commitment to her nation. This experience underscored the challenges women face in traditionally male-dominated fields and cemented her legacy as a trailblazer, inspiring others to persevere even in the face of adversity.

Even after her tenure in politics, Dr. Arteaga continued to advocate for education and cultural initiatives. She founded the FIDAL Foundation, focusing on the integration and development of education in Latin America. The foundation's projects include awards for the best teachers in Ecuador and Latin America, leadership schools, and STEM initiatives to involve young girls in science and technology.

Dr. Arteaga's commitment to lifelong learning is evident in her endeavors. She holds a doctoral law degree, has studied journalism and anthropology, and is currently learning French to better engage with African communities. Her continuous journey in learning exemplifies the importance of staying prepared for new opportunities.

> **"Being proactive means not just seizing opportunities, but also cultivating the patience to build meaningful connections and the foresight to know when to advance and when to pause."**
>
> KangSan Kim (Antonio Stark)

KangSan Kim, also known as Antonio Stark, exemplifies the essence of proactivity in the aerospace sector. His journey is marked by strategic foresight, cultural sensitivity, and continuous learning, propelling his career to great heights. Antonio is the Global Alliance Lead at Ispace, Inc.—a multinational lunar transportation and resource development company. He has previously worked with HEO Robotics and Planet Labs, as well as supporting the US State Department in projects in the Indo-Pacific, accumulating a work portfolio across space policy, security, and sustainability. His accolades include the 2024 NSS-ISDC Excellence Award, the 2022 IAF Emerging Space Leader Award, and the 2022 APSCC Young Talent Award.

Antonio's journey into the space sector was sparked by his early love for science fiction, a passion that led him to explore the vast possibilities of space exploration. Inspired by the visionary worlds of Isaac Asimov, Robert Heinlein, and Frank Herber, he believed from a young age that space held the potential to unify humanity and drive groundbreaking innovation. But it was not only fictional worlds that fueled his aspirations—Antonio was driven by a desire to contribute to a future where the impossible could become reality.

While still in high school, Antonio's passion and keen eye for opportunity led him to a NASA contest focused on designing space settlements. Recognizing this contest as more than a school project, he saw it as a chance to prove that someone from South Korea—a country not yet widely recognized for its space industry—could make an impact on the global stage. His team was the first Korean group to enter the competition, and, to his astonishment, they won second place. The following year, fueled by determination, Antonio's team returned and won the grand prize. These successes were not mere strokes of luck but the result of his proactive engagement, dedication, and ability to recognize the contest as a launchpad for future opportunities.

Beyond competitions, Antonio immersed himself in every aspect of space exploration, attending conferences, volunteering, and seeking out mentors. To overcome financial barriers, he created his own scholarship fund through personal outreach, enabling him to pursue his passion without limitation. His efforts led him to collaborate with multiple NGOs in the space sector, including the Space Generation Advisory Council, the International Astronautical Federation, the Space

Foundation, the Moon Village Association, and the Interstellar Foundation, where he built a robust network and expanded his impact.

His global experience—having lived in seven countries and visited over 40—has taught him the importance of cultural sensitivity in networking. He shares, "Having lived and worked across diverse cultural landscapes, I've learned the delicate art of navigating through varied social and professional etiquettes. In a world that often values aggressive advancement, I've found strength in patience and the quiet cultivation of relationships. True networking is about respecting cultural nuances and investing time to build trust, not merely seizing opportunities. It's about understanding when to advance and when to pause, ensuring that every connection we make is as strong and meaningful as the bonds between the stars in our galaxy."

This approach to networking emphasizes the importance of building meaningful relationships rather than superficial connections. Stark's patience and respect for cultural differences have allowed him to forge strong, genuine bonds, opening numerous career opportunities. He re-engages in these bonds at every opportunity—either at the many space conferences he attends, or by hosting research projects for others to join.

Antonio's proactive approach also involved attending seminars, expanding his knowledge through strategic networking, and setting ambitious goals.

His dedication to personal growth is evident in his goal to read 100 books every year. By combining his preparation and strategic connections, Antonio has positioned himself to seize opportunities effectively and make lasting contributions to the aerospace industry.

"Grab any opportunity when it comes, even if it's unpaid work. You don't need to know exactly where they are headed. You need to trust the process."

Iroka Chidinma Joy, PhD

Iroka Chidinma Joy, PhD, is an Assistant Director and Head

of the Satellite and Navigation Systems Division in the Engineering and Space Systems Department of the National Space Research and Development Agency (NASRDA), Nigeria's space agency. She holds a PhD in Communication Engineering from Ladoke Akintola University of Technology (LAUTECH), where her research focused on the impact of rain attenuation on communication signals, a crucial area for satellite technology.

Her journey into the space industry is divine and a testament to the power of awareness and seizing opportunities. Initially, she aimed to study architecture but switched to electrical and electronics engineering due to family advice. This pivot, though unexpected, set the stage for her future accomplishments. While studying at a polytechnic, a university that provides hands-on, practical, and applied education in STEM fields, Iroka recognized the importance of leveraging every educational opportunity. She completed her youth service and began working with the Nigerian Postal Service but did not stop there.

Iroka's big breakthrough came when she observed a competitive exam for a position at the National Space Research and Development Agency (NASRDA) in Nigeria. By staying informed and recognizing this opportunity, she was able to transition into the space industry. Her proactive approach led her to be part of a team of Nigerian engineers trained at Surrey Satellite Technology Ltd. in the UK, where she contributed to the design, building, and testing of Nigerian satellites (NigSat-2 and NigSat-X) launched in 2011.

Despite being among the few women in her field, Iroka continuously sought ways to grow. She wrote her master's thesis on *The Quantification of the Influence of Rain Attenuation on Received Power at Ka Band*, and led a team to work on the PalmSat-Nig S-Band Microwave Beacon. Her dedication to research and continuous learning propelled her career forward.

Iroka also took advantage of every opportunity to volunteer and educate others. She co-founded and serves as Secretary General of Women in Aerospace Nigeria (WIAN), an organization that visits schools to encourage girls to pursue

STEM careers. Her efforts in promoting STEM education and space science have made her a role model and mentor for Africa's next generation of space leaders. She's also a co-convener of the African Strategy on Fundamental and Applied Physics (ASFAP) on Women in Physics and Community Engagement areas.

Her story exemplifies the importance of awareness and seizing opportunities. By staying informed, volunteering for challenging projects, and committing to continuous learning, Dr. Iroka transformed her career and significantly contributed to the space industry in Nigeria, Africa, and the world at large.

Transforming Insights Into Action

In the vast expanse of your career, each lesson serves as a guiding star, illuminating paths toward personal and professional growth. To truly thrive, it is not enough to understand these lessons; real transformation occurs when you take action.

Start by embracing a **growth mindset**. Cultivate the belief that you can grow through dedication and hard work. This mindset unlocks your potential to innovate and approach challenges with fresh perspectives. **Stephen Covey's** *The 7 Habits of Highly Effective People* offers timeless principles to help you strengthen this mindset and enhance personal effectiveness. Consider starting a journal to document moments of growth and reflect on how these experiences shape your journey.

Next, **reframe challenges as opportunities**. Instead of shying away from difficulties, view them as stepping stones to success. Reflect on a recent challenge and how it allowed you to learn a new skill, forge a meaningful connection, or gain a deeper understanding of your field. **Taylor Brooks' TEDx talk** offers insightful perspectives on making the most of every opportunity, helping you turn adversity into an advantage.

Set clear **career goals** and define the steps needed to achieve them. Regular self-reflection helps ensure you are on the right path, making informed decisions about your future.

Be **proactive** in transforming your career. Take control of your circumstances and anticipate challenges to ensure continuous forward movement. Seek new responsibilities and expand your professional network to stay ahead of industry trends. A valuable resource for building connections is **Opportunity for Youth (OFY)** on LinkedIn, which curates fellowships, scholarships, and internships to help young professionals make an impact. Set a goal to connect with one new person each week; these interactions can become the building blocks of your professional growth.

Commit to lifelong learning by developing a structured learning plan for six months. Identify key areas for improvement and select relevant courses or conferences. Resources like **MIT OpenCourseWare** offer a wealth of materials on various subjects. At the same time, the **UNODC Global eLearning Platform** provides free courses on niche topics like space law and the sustainability of outer space activities. For leadership insights, **Jim Collins's** *Good to Great* explores how leaders make strategic decisions that position them at the forefront of their industries.

Take on challenging assignments, even without immediate reward, to accelerate your growth. Volunteer for projects that push your limits and provide valuable experience. For women in STEM, **TechWomen**, an initiative by the US Department of State, empowers female leaders by providing access to leadership and growth opportunities. These projects and initiatives will enrich your career and broaden your horizons.

As you grow, **engage in professional development activities** such as workshops, networking events, or mentorship to further solidify your progress. These activities provide fresh insights, expand your knowledge, and connect you with others who can offer guidance and support. **The Google Public Policy Fellowship** is an excellent example for those interested in public policy work across various global markets. Additionally, **IBM and Coursera's Generative AI for Executives course** is ideal for leaders looking to integrate AI strategically into their operations.

Document your progress as a powerful motivator. Each small step forward is a victory and a testament to your growth. Start a success journal where you can record these milestones and revisit them regularly to remind yourself how far you have come. Public speaking and personal branding are critical aspects of this process. **Sadaf Tahir's TEDx talk on crafting an effective resume** is a great resource to help you stand out in the job market. Maintaining an updated LinkedIn profile and resume is crucial to showcasing your continuous growth and readiness for new challenges.

Embracing the unknown is not just about confronting fear—it is about opening the door to new possibilities and growth. The courage to enter uncharted territory fuels innovation and drives personal and professional transformation. By continuously learning from setbacks and celebrating even small victories, we can turn uncertainty into a powerful catalyst for progress.

As you move forward, remember that the journey through the unknown is where true discovery happens. Explore beyond your comfort zone, knowing that each step taken with curiosity and determination brings you closer to your greatest achievements.

References

Brooks, T. (2013, October 14). *Taking advantage of opportunities: Taylor Brooks at TEDxRockyViewSchoolsED*. YouTube. https://www.youtube.com/watch?v=kSX0XU2VZTA.

Collins, J. C. (2001). *Good to great: Why some companies make the leap . . . and others don't*. HarperCollins.

Coursera. (n.d.). *Generative A.I. for executives and business leaders course (IBM)*. Coursera. Retrieved September 19, 2024, from https://www.coursera.org/learn/generative-ai-for-executives-business-leaders.

Covey, S. R., & Covey, S. (2020). *The 7 habits of highly effective people: Powerful lessons in personal change*. Simon & Schuster.

Google Policy Fellowship. (n.d.). *Google public policy fellowship*. Google. https://www.google.com/policyfellowship/.

Isaacson, W. (2012, April). The real leadership lessons of Steve Jobs. *Harvard Business Review*. https://hbr.org/2012/04/the-real-leadership-lessons-of-steve-jobs.

Nobel Prize Organization. (n.d.) *Marie Curie: Biographical*. NobelPrize.org. https://www.nobelprize.org/prizes/physics/1903/marie-curie/biographical/.

MIT OpenCourseWare. (2001). *Info*. MIT Open Learning. Retrieved September 19, 2024, from https://ocw.mit.edu/about/.

Opportunities for Youth. (n.d.). http://www.opportunitiesforyouth.org/.

Tahir, S. (2022, November 18). *Make your resume talk for you, Sadaf Tahir, TEDxNainiStudio*. YouTube. https://www.youtube.com/watch?v=eSU_x4kpTYE.

United Nations Office on Drugs and Crime (UNODC). (n.d.).

UNODC eLearning platform. UNODC Global eLearning. Retrieved March 2024, from https://elearningunodc.org/.

Umoh, R. (2017, December 18). *Billionaire Richard Branson reveals why he's such a huge fan of always saying 'yes.'* CNBC. https://www.cnbc.com/2017/12/18/billionaire-richard-branson-reveals-why-he-always-says-yes.html.

Bureau of Education and Cultural Affairs. (n.d.). *TechWomen*. U.S. Department of State. https://www.techwomen.org/.

CHAPTER TWO DEFYING GRAVITY: TRYING ANYWAY, EVEN WHEN THE ODDS ARE AGAINST YOU

"Success is not measured by how easily we achieve our goals, but by our unwavering determination to try again and again, understanding that failure is just F.A.I.L.—First Attempt In Learning."

Shelli Brunswick

L ife often presents us with seemingly insurmountable challenges, similar to the force of gravity constantly pulling us down. However, adversity reveals our true potential. The journey of defying gravity is not about avoiding obstacles but about embracing them as opportunities to grow, adapt, and persevere. This chapter explores the art of overcoming the odds. Inspiration is provided by the remarkable stories of resilience, adaptability, and the unwavering commitment of José Hernández, SpaceX, and other global thought leaders.

José Hernández, a former NASA astronaut, exemplifies resilience and determination. Hernández, the son of Mexican migrant farmworkers, faced overwhelming odds in his quest to become an astronaut. He applied to NASA's astronaut program 12 times. However, instead of giving up after each rejection, Hernández chose to adapt. He continually improved his qualifications. He learned Russian and obtained a pilot's license, refusing to abandon his dream. In 2004, his perseverance culminated in his selection as part of NASA's 19th class of astronauts. His journey, chronicled in his autobiography *Reaching for the Stars* and the 2022 Netflix film *A Million Miles*

Away, is a testament to the power of adaptability, dedication, and the willingness to take calculated risks to achieve one's goals.

Similarly, SpaceX's journey offers a compelling example of how embracing failure and taking calculated risks can lead to groundbreaking success. Founded by Elon Musk, SpaceX aimed to revolutionize space travel, but the road was far from smooth. In its early years, SpaceX experienced multiple rocket launch failures. The first three launches of their Falcon 1 rocket ended in failure, pushing the company to the brink of bankruptcy. However, instead of giving up, SpaceX viewed these failures as invaluable learning experiences. Each failure provided critical insights, allowing the team to refine their designs and processes.

The fourth launch was successful, making SpaceX the first privately funded company to put a rocket into orbit. This success marked a turning point and set the stage for further innovations. The development of reusable rockets, a core aspect of SpaceX's mission, showcased their commitment to learning from failure. After several spectacular crashes of the Falcon 9 boosters attempting to land, SpaceX achieved a successful landing in December 2015. Today, booster landings are routine, dramatically reducing the cost of space launches and proving the value of persistence and calculated risk-taking.

Elon Musk famously said, "When something is important enough, you do it even if the odds are not in your favor." This mindset is at the heart of SpaceX's success. Musk's willingness to embrace failure as part of the innovation process and his commitment to taking calculated risks have been instrumental in SpaceX's journey from repeated setbacks to groundbreaking achievements.

The stories about José Hernández and SpaceX demonstrate that success is not about avoiding risks or failures but about learning from them, adapting, and pushing forward. These individuals took calculated risks, understanding that achieving extraordinary goals requires stepping into the unknown. They faced the unknown with a plan and a willingness to learn from setbacks. This process of learning from setbacks is not a hindrance but a pathway to success, and this understanding can inspire us all.

As we delve deeper into this chapter, we will explore the insights of diverse global thought leaders who defied the odds, proving that resilience, adaptability, and persistence can transform challenges into remarkable successes. These leaders come from various fields, including business, science, sports, and the arts, and their stories will inspire and motivate you on your own journey. Whether in the space industry or our personal and professional lives, the principles of defying gravity remain the same: embrace challenges, adapt to new circumstances, take calculated risks, and persist with unwavering determination.

Personal Reflections

After completing my bachelor's degree, working as an airman during the day, and taking classes at night and on weekends, I met the requirements to apply to become an officer in the United States Air Force (USAF). However, there was a challenge: the Air Force primarily sought science, technology, engineering, and mathematics (STEM) professionals. I did not fit these criteria, having earned a bachelor's degree in business administration. With a mere 12% acceptance rate, the selection odds were slim. Despite this perceived obstacle, I chose to apply.

I compiled all my transcripts, gathered letters of recommendation, and submitted my application. After months of waiting, I received the news: I was not selected. Disappointed but undeterred, I resubmitted my application for the next officer selection review board. I updated my application to present myself in the best possible light. I contacted the wonderful people who had written my letters of recommendation and asked them to update their letters. I revised my essay and ensured that all information was current.

While waiting for the second selection board results, I began exploring alternative career paths within the Air Force, preparing myself for Plans B, C, and D in case my primary goal didn't come to fruition. When the results of the second selection board arrived, I was overjoyed to learn that I had been selected to become an officer in the USAF.

This experience taught me the invaluable lesson of trying anyway, even when the odds are against you. This lesson underscores the importance of persistence, tenacity, and resilience. Sometimes, achieving your goals requires multiple attempts. Failure is not the end but a catalyst to learn, grow, and develop. This mindset, as encapsulated by Admiral William H. McRaven's words, "The only easy day was yesterday," is a powerful reminder of the importance of continual effort and resilience in daily challenges.

Insights From Global Thought Leaders

"I believe that dreams can come true. It doesn't matter how crazy that dream is or how long it takes to achieve it; with perseverance and patience, if you believe in it, you will achieve it."

Priscilla Nowajewski, PhD

Priscilla Nowajewski's journey into science was sparked by the inspiration she drew from her female Chilean science teachers in high school. Their encouragement and example planted the seed for her aspirations, fueling her desire to become a scientist. Initially hoping to study astronomy, she faced an early setback when she wasn't accepted into her chosen program. Refusing to give up, she enrolled in a physics program instead, continuing to seek out opportunities to work alongside astronomers. By staying committed to her goal and collaborating with experts in the field, she built a solid foundation in astronomy and ultimately found her path in planetary science. Her persistence in facing obstacles exemplifies her determination to succeed.

Priscilla's academic path was laden with challenges. Physics, while a field she felt drawn to, presented numerous difficulties. Completing assignments often took longer for her than for her peers, and the academic environment was both competitive and, at times, unsupportive. Some professors questioned her abilities, casting doubt on her place within the program and creating an isolating experience. Despite giving her best efforts, the mounting obstacles ultimately led her to leave her master's program in physics. Yet, this did not deter her resolve to become a researcher. Instead, Priscilla chose a new path, proving that setbacks are merely setups for a different course to success.

Priscilla's passion for planetary science was reignited at a Committee on Space Research (COSPAR) workshop on Planetary Science in 2007, where she analyzed Mars data to identify dust devil tracks. This experience, along with a Planetary Science course during her master's studies, where she discovered the Hexagon on Saturn's North Pole, cemented her interest in planetary atmospheres. She soon enrolled in a PhD in fluid dynamics, a field that allowed her to explore her passion further. This decision marked a turning point; her studies felt intuitive and fulfilling, validating that she had finally found her calling.

Today, she is a data analyst at the Atacama Large Millimeter/submillimeter Array (ALMA) Observatory in northern Chile. She contributes to groundbreaking discoveries as part of the world's most advanced astronomical observatory. Her journey to planetary science is one of resilience, unwavering commitment, and a powerful reminder that success is not always a direct path, but a journey shaped by persistence.

Priscilla often shares a simple yet impactful piece of advice with her students and proteges: "Try anyway, even when the odds are against you." Much like the celestial bodies she studies, her journey shines as a beacon for future generations. Inspired by her high school mentors and by pushing beyond the obstacles, Priscilla's story continues to inspire, shaping the future of planetary science in Chile and beyond.

"In the tapestry of innovation, each thread of failure is a lesson leading us to greater understanding. Practice taking risks to sharpen your intuition and learn quickly from your failures."

Ben Haldeman

Ben Haldeman's career showcases the power of taking risks,

embracing failure, and evolving beyond technical achievements into visionary pursuits. Fascinated by building from a young age, Ben studied mechanical engineering at Penn State and Berkeley. His early work on instruments to search for life on Mars ignited his curiosity about the universe, and his technical skills flourished in developing telescopes and satellites. However, Ben's journey goes beyond engineering and into profound personal growth, where he came to view space exploration not only as a technical endeavor but as a deeply human one.

Ben's time at Planet Labs, where he helped build over 300 small satellites to image Earth daily, opened his eyes to the interconnection between humanity and space. Through this work, he began to see Earth as a living organism, inspiring him to think about the broader role of humanity as stewards of life. This shift in perspective was catalyzed during an ayahuasca ceremony in Guatemala, where Ben envisioned Earth's purpose as an organism with a drive to reproduce life. He came to see humanity's mission as a cosmic legacy bearer, tasked with carrying Earth's genetic heritage into space. This revelation led him to create LifeShip, a company dedicated to preserving Earth's genetic material and biodiversity by storing DNA in space to ensure the survival of life in the face of potential catastrophic disasters.

LifeShip's mission reflects Ben's holistic approach to life and space exploration. The initiative aims to create a "backup" for Earth by placing miniaturized DNA banks on the Moon, marking the first steps in carrying the seeds of Earth's life beyond our planet. For Ben, this project aligns with his vision of a future where humanity harmonizes with life on Earth and expands this stewardship to other worlds, actively preserving and spreading life across the cosmos.

In the traditionally risk-averse space industry, Ben has embraced an iterative, high-risk approach often seen in the tech world. He reframed failure as a critical learning tool, sharpening his ability to assess and manage risks while pushing the boundaries of space technology. His work at Planet Labs exemplifies this philosophy. Building these satellites involved numerous setbacks; many of the early satellites did not perform as expected. However, each failure offered valuable insights, leading to improvements in later generations of satellites. Eventually, Planet Lab's agile approach led to the development of small satellites that outperformed much larger and more costly ones, enabling daily imaging of Earth. This breakthrough transformed the aerospace industry.

Beyond technical accomplishments, Ben's journey has evolved into one of holistic leadership. He has become a leader who values personal connections, seeing work and life as deeply interconnected. His experiences as a professional cyclist and big-wall rock climber, including speed-climbing the 3,000-foot face of El Capitan in under 24 hours, honed his intuition around fear and risk. These pursuits taught him the importance of quick decision-making and balancing risk with caution, skills that have proven invaluable in his career and life.

From building telescopes to envisioning life among the stars, Ben's journey is a testament to the power of moving quickly, taking risks, and learning from failure. His work reminds us that success is more than technical prowess—it is about recognizing our shared responsibility to safeguard life on Earth and carry its legacy forward. By integrating this passion for space with a commitment to life's preservation, Ben's story inspires us all to look beyond the stars and consider our place within the cosmos.

"You don't know until you try. Some people think I apply for too many things. An important aspect for me is documenting the entire process because it really helps monitor your growth. Always be looking for opportunities and then give it a shot because you never know what's in store for you. Also, simply applying gives the organizations access to you as you become part of their database. The space community is very close-knit, and that's why your efforts at the end of the day will get noticed, and things will fall into place."

Sejal Budholiya

Sejal Budholiya's journey in the space industry highlights the significance of celebrating small wins and finding meaning along the way. Growing up in India, Sejal's fascination with the stars led her to pursue mechanical and aerospace engineering. While her path into engineering may seem straightforward, she faced significant academic and societal challenges. In her school years, Sejal struggled with mathematics, a critical skill for her future career in aerospace. Despite the doubts voiced by those around her, who questioned whether she could succeed in engineering without excelling in math, Sejal remained determined. With the support of a dedicated teacher who valued her problem-solving attempts over immediate success, she gradually transformed a major weakness into a strength, building the confidence that would later fuel her accomplishments in engineering.

Sejal also confronted societal expectations regarding gender roles. Entering the male-dominated field of mechanical engineering, she often faced skepticism about her abilities. Many questioned whether a woman could excel in such a discipline, but these doubts only fueled her determination. Sejal's experience of being one of the few women in her field, both during her studies and in her professional role, presented unique challenges. Refusing to be discouraged, she sought out mentors and expanded her network, finding support through formal mentorship programs like the United Nations Office for Outer Space Affairs Space4Women program. Her experience of breaking barriers as a woman in STEM demonstrates that setbacks are simply opportunities in disguise, leading to growth and innovation.

Mentorship has been a cornerstone of Sejal's journey, offering her guidance and a lifeline during her most challenging moments. She credits her mentors with helping her recognize her potential and transform obstacles into springboards. Her mentors offered more than advice—they provided unwavering support and pushed her to explore new opportunities and reach beyond her comfort zone. Her participation in formal mentorship programs has been transformative, offering her a sense of belonging, purpose, and the courage to build meaningful connections. Through these relationships, Sejal has learned to balance the demands of life while pursuing her dreams with passion and perseverance.

Beyond her professional accomplishments, Sejal's love for dance has been a constant throughout her life. She co-founded a nonprofit organization, Project Neysa, to provide free dance classes to underprivileged children, using her passion for dance as a way to give back to her community. For Sejal, dance is a bridge that connects diverse communities, offering a sense of fulfillment and purpose. She believes giving back can be achieved through one's passions, enriching both personal and community growth.

Throughout her career, Sejal has been involved in innovative projects addressing societal issues. She has earned patents for designs, such as a modular rainwater harvesting system that uses traditional techniques to improve water management in rural areas. During the COVID-19 pandemic, she developed a combined bed and stretcher assembly to help alleviate medical equipment shortages. Sejal's engineering solutions, often inspired by nature, aim to positively impact society.

Sejal's story underscores the importance of empathy, open-mindedness, and embracing diverse perspectives. She inspires others to pursue their dreams and drive meaningful change in the world by fostering genuine human connections rooted in shared passions.

Transforming Insights Into Action

Defying gravity—whether in your career or personal life —is about embracing challenges, learning from setbacks, and remaining committed to your goals despite the odds. **Adaptation and learning** are essential, as each failure becomes an opportunity for growth. When faced with obstacles, take the time to analyze setbacks, make the necessary adjustments, and keep moving forward. Flexibility, combined with the willingness to embrace change, turns challenges into opportunities for success. As highlighted in *Lunar Legacy: DNA of Success* by Greg S. Reid and Ben Haldeman, successful individuals often leverage their failures to propel themselves toward greater achievements.

At the core of this journey is **commitment to your goals**. Persistence and resilience are key to overcoming obstacles. No matter how challenging the path may seem, staying focused and dedicated will eventually lead to success. *Elon Musk: Tesla, SpaceX, and the Quest for a Fantastic Future* by Ashlee Vance offers a powerful reminder of how staying committed to seemingly impossible goals can lead to groundbreaking innovations. Musk's journey, like your own, involves taking **calculated risks**. Researching thoroughly, analyzing potential outcomes, and preparing contingency plans is essential. These steps help ensure that taking risks fosters innovation and leads to meaningful achievements.

Along the way, remember to **celebrate small wins**. Each small victory builds momentum, keeping you motivated. Recognizing these achievements helps you maintain perspective and push you toward your larger goals. **Finding meaning in the journey** is just as valuable as reaching the destination. Pursuing your goals allows for personal growth, new experiences, and the development of relationships. *Make Your Bed* by William H. McRaven reinforces this concept by emphasizing how small, consistent actions can create lasting change.

To bring these lessons to life, set specific, measurable, achievable, relevant, and time-bound (**SMART**) **goals**. Surround yourself with a **support system** that believes in you and encourages your efforts. Mentors who have faced similar challenges can offer invaluable guidance, helping you navigate through tough times with their wisdom and experience. *I Am Malala,* a book by Malala Yousafzai and Christina Lamb, is a powerful example of mentorship and resilience. Malala's determination to pursue her education despite adversity underscores the power of resilience and community support.

Each setback is not a stumbling block but a **springboard**

for greater success. Use failure as a tool for **continuous improvement** and adaptation rather than a reason to give up. Lifelong learning is critical to thriving in any environment. Whether you're learning about **risk-taking** through resources like Beatrice Gauthier's *Taking Risks: Our Favorite Reads* or exploring innovative problem-solving methods from thought leaders like José Hernández in his TEDxPolanco talk, *Alcanzando las estrellas*, you'll find that continuous growth is integral to achieving success.

Lastly, dare to take that leap. Choose a challenge that previously intimidated you and plan to tackle it head-on. Whether it's a new project, a leadership role, or an initiative to bring about change, let today be the day you take the first step. The Netflix film *A Million Miles Away*, about José Hernández's journey to become an astronaut, shows how each step taken with perseverance and courage leads to remarkable heights. By **persisting with resilience**, seeking out support, and celebrating each achievement along the way, you'll transform obstacles into opportunities, ultimately defying the gravitational pull of doubt and fear.

Through these actions, you can achieve remarkable things —turning failures into fuel for success and transforming your journey into a testament to perseverance. The key is to **try anyway**, even when the odds seem stacked against you. By believing in yourself, learning from failure, and pushing forward with determination, you create a trajectory toward success that knows no bounds. Your journey is yours to define, and with every step, you'll defy gravity, moving ever closer to your dreams.

References

Bergin, C. (2008, September 28). *Space X's Falcon I launch success on fourth attempt.* NASA SpaceFlight.com.https://www.nasaspaceflight.com/2008/09/live-space-xs-falcon-i-to-make-fourth-attempt-for-success/.

Economy, P. (2024, June 1). 19 Elon Musk quotes that will inspire you to success. *Inc. Magazine.* https://www.inc.com/peter-economy/19-elon-musk-quotes-for-success.html.

Gauthier, B. (2023, August 16). Taking risks: Our favorite reads. *Harvard Business Review.* https://hbr.org/2023/08/taking-risks-our-favorite-reads.

Hernández, J. M. (2012). *Reaching for the stars: The inspiring story of a migrant farmworker turned astronaut.* Center Street.

Hernandez, J. (2017, June). *Alcanzando las estrellas* [Video]. TED Conferences. https://www.ted.com/talks/jose_hernandez_alcanzando_las_estrellas?delay=5s&subtitle=en.

Marquez Abella, A. (Director). (2023). *A million miles away* [Film]. Amazon MGM Studios Select Films. https://press.amazonmgmstudios.com/us/en/original-movies/a-million-miles-away.

McRaven, W. H. (2017). *Make your bed: Little things that can change your life . . . And maybe the world.* Grand Central Publishing.

Reid, G. S., & Haldeman, B. (2024). *Lunar legacy: DNA of success.* Joint Venture Publishing, Blue Sky.

SpaceRef. (2008, September 29). *SpaceX Successfully Launches Falcon 1 to Orbit.* SpaceNews.com. https://spacenews.com/spacex-successfully-launches-falcon-1-to-orbit/.

Vance, A. (2017). *Elon Musk: Tesla, SpaceX, and the quest for a fantastic future*. HarperCollins.

Yousafzai, M., & McCormick, P. (2016). *I am Malala: How one girl stood up for education and changed the world* (Young Readers Edition). Little, Brown Books for Young Readers.

CHAPTER THREE EMBRACING THE UNCHARTED COSMOS: CONQUERING FEAR OF THE UNKNOWN

"Embrace the unknown as the canvas of possibility—where the absence of predetermined paths opens the door to create and influence the future with our actions."

Shelli Brunswick

T he vastness of space, a symbol of the unknown, is a realm that offers both limitless possibilities and demanding challenges. Similarly, our personal and professional lives often present us with situations, opportunities, and unfamiliar, potentially intimidating obstacles. However, these uncertainties sow the seeds of growth, innovation, and transformation, empowering us to shape our destinies.

Historian Laurel Thatcher Ulrich once remarked, "Well-behaved women seldom make history." This powerful quote reminds us that stepping beyond the conventional and embracing the unknown is essential for making significant and lasting impacts. Whether navigating the depths of space or the complexities of our lives, the courage to venture into the unknown allows us to conquer fears and thrive in uncertain environments, showcasing our resilience and bravery.

The unknown can be daunting, but it is also an invitation to create, innovate, and influence our future. Just as space exploration pushes the boundaries of human knowledge, embracing uncharted territories in our lives can lead to life-changing experiences. By shifting our perspective, we can view uncertainty not as a barrier but as an opportunity—a blank canvas on which to paint our dreams and aspirations. This reinvention is not just a possibility but a power we all possess.

This mindset is crucial for leaders across all fields, not just for explorers or visionaries. Nelson Mandela's life embodies this ethos; he transformed a nation, not by avoiding fear but by confronting it. He poignantly stated, "I learned that courage was not the absence of fear but the triumph over it. The brave man is not he who does not feel afraid, but he who conquers that fear." Mandela's journey from imprisonment to the presidency is a testament to the courage required to face the unknown and transform fear into a catalyst for change.

Similarly, innovators like Steve Jobs exemplify the importance of embracing risk and curiosity. His philosophy, "Stay hungry. Stay foolish." fueled revolutionary technologies that reshaped entire industries. By constantly challenging the status quo and embracing the unknown, Jobs led Apple to unprecedented success, proving that outstanding achievements often lie beyond our comfort zones.

The Voyager missions are a profound example of this spirit in space exploration. Initially launched to explore the outer planets, these missions have since ventured into interstellar space, far beyond their original destinations. They embody the essence of exploration and discovery, reminding us that embracing the unknown is about reaching new destinations and expanding our horizons in ways we never imagined.

Similarly, in the broader context of space exploration, companies like Toyota are venturing into unknown territories by developing the Lunar Cruiser to traverse the Moon and potentially Mars. This project, part of a larger initiative to expand human presence in space, is a testament to the power of embracing the unknown. Parallel to commercial initiatives, NASA's Artemis program aims to return humans to the Moon and establish a sustainable presence by the late 2020s, paving the way for manned missions to Mars. Brimming with complexities and uncharted technical challenges, this program embodies the essence of confronting and mastering the unknown.

As we delve deeper into this chapter, we will explore stories of individuals who have thrived by embracing the unknown. Their journeys offer invaluable lessons, showing us how to confront our fears, harness the potential of uncertainty, and unlock the catalytic power of the uncharted cosmos. Through these narratives, may you find inspiration to navigate your own "uncharted cosmos," daring to dream, explore, and ultimately conquer. Remember, every setback is a setup for a comeback, and every challenge is an opportunity for growth.

Personal Reflections

One pivotal lesson I've embraced throughout my career is, "Don't Fear the Unknown." When I was selected to become an Air Force officer, the assignment was not what I had hoped for— I was chosen to be a space acquisition officer, a role I knew nothing about and initially did not want. I had envisioned myself as a personnel officer on a familiar and comfortable path, surrounded by colleagues I knew well.

With deep reservations about this new career path, I contacted several mentors, hoping they could help me shift my trajectory from space acquisition to personnel. Despite numerous efforts, I eventually received a decisive call from the Air Force Personnel Center. The voice on the other end informed me, "Sergeant Brunswick, the Air Force needs you to be a space acquisition officer." At that moment, I accepted the assignment with a firm "Yes, sir," and a sincere "Thank you." That response began a pivotal chapter in my life, leading to my 25-year career in the space industry.

This experience taught me an invaluable lesson: embrace new opportunities, be adaptable, and step out of your comfort zone. Instead of fearing the unfamiliar, shift your perspective, and view it as an opportunity to grow and broaden your horizons.

My journey and these expansive ventures into space

underscore a shared truth: navigating the unknown, whether in career shifts or lunar explorations, opens up new frontiers and possibilities. It's about transforming apprehension into opportunity, which is essential for innovation and progress.

Insights From Global Thought Leaders

"Creativity flourishes in the absence of fear, transforming barriers into bridges. When we release the constraints of doubt and embrace the possibilities of 'what if,' we unlock the full spectrum of our imagination, inviting innovation to take flight. Let's create a sanctuary for our ideas, where curiosity replaces fear and every 'failure' is a stepping stone towards success."

Michelle Del Valle

Michelle Del Valle's story is a remarkable journey of curiosity, courage, and innovation, illustrating how embracing the unknown can lead to extraordinary outcomes. Growing up in Texas, Michelle's fascination with science was evident early on. Her academic pursuits in biomedical engineering laid a strong foundation, yet her leap into the aerospace industry marked a pivotal turn in her career.

During her journey from big pharma to real estate to aerospace, Michelle connected with influential figures. One was the VP of her old department in big pharma, who shared advice that helped Michelle tackle fear.

The VP's response became a pivotal moment in Michelle's professional development. She shared a metaphor that would stick with Michelle permanently: when deeply engaged in problem-solving, one's glasses become covered in dirt, obscuring the ability to celebrate achievements. The VP then shared a personal story about her own PhD journey, where her brother had offered similar wisdom. He had advised her to print and display even a single correct graph during her research struggles—a small but significant victory. This simple act of celebrating one defendable result became her way of "wiping the mess shit off her glasses" and acknowledging progress, eventually leading to her successful PhD completion and a position as VP at a Fortune 500 pharmaceutical company.

Michelle's story reflects a characteristic pattern in her approach to challenges. Her fearlessness in self-advocacy and her previous accomplishments propelled her to lead many interdisciplinary innovation efforts, while her passion for complex problem-solving helped her overcome initial self-doubt—the kind that typically prevents others from taking their moonshot. Her remarkable drive and self-motivation continually led her toward ambitious challenges filled with uncertainty. For Michelle, fear manifests not in the moment but during the challenge, particularly concerning how the time required to solve challenges impacts team goals and timelines. Her instinct to push through consecutive challenges without pausing to celebrate successes along the way often resulted in a muddied perspective, limiting her ability to approach problems with fresh insights and celebrate wins with herself and the team.

This wisdom encapsulates a powerful lesson about the importance of maintaining perspective and celebrating incremental progress while pursuing ambitious goals. Through the VP's mentorship, Michelle learned that success isn't solely measured by achieving the ultimate objective, but also by recognizing and appreciating the smaller victories along the journey.

This realization marked the start of a significant mindset shift. Michelle actively began to counteract the fear of not having enough time by celebrating successes as an essential part of growth, a catalyst that, when embraced, could lead her to make bold, innovative choices. By reframing each challenge as an opportunity to expand her boundaries, she empowered herself to take risks that propelled her forward. Through intentional practice, Michelle adopted a perspective where failures became valuable learning experiences that should be celebrated, essential for achieving lasting success. Her willingness to confront fear head-on enabled her to thrive in the aerospace industry and led to groundbreaking advancements and solutions.

Her entrepreneurial spirit drove Michelle to establish FinSat, a company dedicated to creating sustainable urban infrastructure that honors cultural history while addressing climate risk. This venture goes beyond profit, striving for systemic improvements that benefit communities on multiple levels. Michelle's love of challenge and facing fear has taken her on a journey of learning and building across industries and regions. Her curiosity and mindset have led her to speak at international and domestic conferences, from Davos to Seattle, manage a real estate portfolio, promote global space education through multiple philanthropic contributions, and she now happily runs a multinational company that focuses on climate risk for urban revitalization. Her efforts have propelled her ventures and influenced the broader landscape of space exploration, real estate, pharmaceuticals, and urban development.

Her journey underscores the importance of adopting a mindset that views the unknown not as a barrier but as a gateway to new opportunities and successes. Michelle's story serves as a beacon for those standing at the edge of their familiar worlds, contemplating the leap into new endeavors. By maintaining an open mind and fostering curiosity, she demonstrates that the unknown can be a landscape ripe with potential rather than a void of fear. Michelle's visionary outlook and transformative projects inspire and lead the way toward a more innovative and sustainable future.

"Uncertainty is an inherent trait of the future."

Roger Spitz

Growing up in South Africa, Roger Spitz's curiosity about how societies transform and adapt was deeply influenced by the country's socio-political landscape. Living through South Africa's transition from apartheid to democracy, he witnessed firsthand the resilience and adaptability required for meaningful change. This period of seismic shifts—politically, socially, and economically—became a springboard for Roger's fascination with systemic change, prompting him to question the structures that underpin societies and economies. He observed the contrasts between outdated governance models and the adaptability of communities determined to progress, realizing a critical need for flexible, resilient frameworks that could endure and evolve. This experience laid the foundation for his later work, where he champions systemic change as essential for thriving in complexity and uncertainty.

Fueled by this curiosity, Roger pursued studies in economics and finance in the United Kingdom, driven by a desire to explore these dynamics on a global scale. He earned his Master's in Corporate & International Finance from the University of Durham and qualified as a Chartered Accountant with the Institute of Chartered Accountants in England & Wales.

After completing his studies, Roger embarked on a successful career in investment banking, ultimately leading Global Technology Mergers & Acquisitions (M&A) at BNP Paribas. Over two decades, he advised on over 50 transactions totaling $25 billion, guiding companies through strategic decisions, such as M&A and initial public offerings (IPO). In these roles, Roger led investment banking businesses in London, Paris, and later San Francisco, advising CEOs, founders, and boards globally while evaluating companies, competitiveness, and disruptive technologies.

Despite his professional success, Roger began to feel that his work lacked a higher purpose and a deeper impact aligned with his interest in systemic change. The career stability he had built in investment banking no longer fulfilled his vision of meaningful contribution. In 2017, Roger relocated to San Francisco, California, immersing himself in new intellectual ecosystems, think tanks, and academic organizations. He deepened his understanding of complexity science and systems thinking, futures studies and strategic foresight, artificial intelligence, and emerging technologies. This exploration phase reignited his passion for existential philosophy, particularly ideas around agency and uncertainty, which resonated with his professional journey and personal insights.

By 2019, Roger had charted a new path more aligned with his vision of addressing systemic challenges and anticipating disruption. He founded Techistential, a foresight practice that advises CEOs, founders, and boards on strategy in uncertainty, preparing them for disruptions and helping create sustainable value. This work inspired the creation of the Disruptive Futures Institute, a think tank dedicated to researching and thriving on disruption, offering thought leadership, education, and research on how organizations can adapt to an increasingly complex and unpredictable world.

Roger's work is deeply influenced by existential philosophy, which explores meaning and purpose in human existence. Drawing on thinkers like Jean-Paul Sartre, Roger believes that our actions shape our reality and that we can actively engage with the unknown to shape our future, rather than passively observing it. This belief underpins his approach to strategic foresight, encouraging leaders to embrace uncertainty and use it as a springboard for systems innovation.

Today, as the President of Techistential and Chairman of the Disruptive Futures Institute, Roger continues to influence global thought leadership on foresight, innovation, and sustainability. His books, *Disrupt With Impact* and *The Definitive Guide to Thriving on Disruption*, encapsulate his methods, offering leaders and organizations a guide to navigating the complexities of a rapidly changing world. He is passionate about education, which is the strongest lever to drive systems change, and is on the Board of the non-profit Teach the Future which offers futures thinking education programs for young students globally. Roger's journey is a testament to the power of embracing the unknown and thriving in the face of disruption.

"Nothing is unchangeable. You can make a shift."

Stela Lupushor

Stela Lupushor's journey from the Soviet Union to becoming

a visionary leader in workforce strategy and technology integration is defined by adaptability and a fearless embrace of new opportunities. Born in the Soviet Union and later a citizen of Moldova, Stela experienced the dramatic upheaval of the Soviet Union's dissolution, the unbundling of the economic ties with other former republics, and the total collapse of Moldova's economy, which transformed her personal and professional lives. As Moldova transitioned to independence, Stela had the opportunity to join country-wide efforts to privatize state-owned enterprises and build the capital markets infrastructure. This experience taught her early on that change is the only constant, and that uncertainty can lead to significant growth if approached with an open mind.

Throughout her journey, simple questions like "Would you like to go?" or "Would you like to try?" opened doors that shaped her career, inviting her to explore uncharted territories and take on roles she had not initially imagined. These early experiences fueled Stela's interest in systemic change and adaptability. Her work took her to Ukraine and Russia, where she continued leading complex transformation projects, ultimately landing her in the US, where she encountered a whole new set of challenges and opportunities. Through each move, she learned to navigate different cultures, systems, and ways of thinking, embracing a mindset of flexibility and continuous learning. Stela's personal journey taught her that no path is unchangeable and that, by leaning into the unknown, she could find opportunities to impact not only her career but also the broader landscape of workforce strategy and innovation.

Stela attributes much of her success to embracing uncertainty and trusting in the timing of opportunities. Reflecting on her unique background, she says, "I grew up in a country that doesn't exist. I spoke a language that no longer exists. Nothing is unchangeable. You can make a shift. Look forward to what is coming." This perspective, combined with humility and curiosity, has guided her through various challenges and opportunities.

One of Stela's key contributions is her enthusiasm for the global space ecosystem and its potential to drive innovation and job creation. She teaches digital workplace design and design thinking as an adjunct professor at New York University's School of Professional Studies. She created a Mars colony case study to inspire her students to think beyond earthly realities and innovate employment experiences for future space settlements. Her holistic approach encourages forward-thinking solutions that can also reshape today's workplace.

Stela is also passionate about removing barriers that prevent women and minorities from pursuing meaningful employment. She focuses on ageism, particularly for women over 45 re-entering the workforce after career breaks. She founded a nonprofit that addresses career breaks, skills gaps, and outdated networks, aiming to change perceptions of older women in the workplace and highlight their wisdom, intelligence, and energy.

Believing that systemic changes can improve job prospects for underrepresented groups, Stela emphasizes the importance of collaboration between all stakeholders. Her journey exemplifies a fearless embrace of the unknown and highlights how building strong relationships and seizing new opportunities are essential to personal and professional growth.

Transforming Insights Into Action

In this chapter, we explored how embracing the unknown can fuel both personal and professional growth. Let's turn these concepts into practical ideas that you can incorporate into your everyday life, thereby reducing the fear and excitement associated with uncertainty.

One powerful way to manage fear is by **reframing it as excitement**. When faced with unfamiliar challenges, fear is a natural response. But what if you could transform that fear into something positive? Fear and excitement are physically similar —both increase your heart rate and heighten your senses. So, the next time you feel anxiety creeping in, remind yourself that this is your body gearing up for a new adventure. By shifting your mindset, you'll approach new opportunities with curiosity rather than hesitation. In her TED Talk, *Your Elusive Creative Genius,* Elizabeth Gilbert touches on how embracing the unknown can nurture creativity and open doors to new possibilities.

Challenging assumptions is another critical step. We spark new ideas when we regularly question our beliefs and ask, "Why?" or "What if?" This practice leads to creativity and opens up space for breakthroughs. In *The Definitive Guide to Thriving on Disruption,* Roger Spitz emphasizes the importance of questioning the status quo to foster innovation. By challenging what we think we know, we make room for unexpected solutions to emerge.

Embracing change as an opportunity for growth is equally important. The world is in constant motion, and adaptability has become essential. Whether it's a career shift, new technology, or simply a change in routine, these moments offer a chance to evolve. Nelson Mandela's *Long Walk to Freedom* illustrates this beautifully, as his life is a testament to the power of accepting and adapting to change. Mandela's ability to see beyond obstacles and embrace transformation is a reminder that change brings new opportunities.

Innovation requires boldness—an openness to experiment and try new approaches. The unknown is the birthplace of creativity, and being willing to explore unconventional ideas can lead to significant progress. Anna Tavis and Stela Lupushor, in *Humans at Work: The Art and Practice of Creating the Hybrid Workplace,* underscore the need for innovative thinking in today's rapidly evolving environments. When you're unafraid to push the limits and test new ideas, you open the door to breakthroughs.

Learning from setbacks is another essential component of growth. Every challenge offers a lesson, and reflecting on what went wrong allows you to refine your approach. Resilience is built through this process of reflection and adjustment. The University of Pennsylvania's *Resilience Skills in a Time of*

Uncertainty provides valuable strategies for bouncing back from setbacks and thriving amidst uncertainty. The more we learn from our mistakes, the stronger and more adaptable we become.

Curiosity is a powerful driver of growth, keeping us open to new experiences and knowledge. By cultivating curiosity, we constantly expand our horizons and sharpen our skills. Michelle Del Valle's *IgnitedThinkers* podcast showcases how curiosity can ignite new passions and push us beyond our comfort zones. It encourages us to keep asking questions and never stop learning.

Finally, **celebrating the unknown** can transform how we perceive uncertainty. Instead of fearing the unknown, we can see it as a new opportunity. The unknown holds the potential for discovery, growth, and innovation. By approaching it with an open heart and mind, we unlock some of the most rewarding experiences of our lives.

When you apply these insights, you'll find that the unknown is not a barrier—it is an invitation. It is a space where creativity thrives, growth happens, and you can challenge yourself to reach new heights. So, as you face uncertainty in the future, remember that within it lies the potential for your greatest achievements.

References

Del Valle, M. (2024, March 11). *Michelle Del Valle: Founder and CEO of FinSat* [Video]. YouTube. https://www.youtube.com/watch?v=DNEcLXMqzZc.

Gilbert, E. (2009, February 8). *Elizabeth Gilbert: Your elusive creative genius* [Video]. TED Conferences. https://www.ted.com/talks/elizabeth_gilbert_your_elusive_creative_genius?subtitle=en.

Jet Propulsion Laboratory, California Institute of Technology. (n.d.) *Voyager mission overview.* NASA. https://science.nasa.gov/mission/voyager/mission-overview.

Jobs, S. (2008, March 8). *Steve Jobs' 2005 Stanford commencement address* [Video]. YouTube. https://www.youtube.com/watch?v=UF8uR6Z6KLc.

Mandela, N. (n.d.). *Quotable Quote.* Goodreads. Retrieved September 19, 2024, from https://www.goodreads.com/quotes/5156-i-learned-that-courage-was-not-the-absence-of-fear.

Mandela, N. (1995). *Long walk to freedom.* Little, Brown.

NASA. (n.d.). *Humans in space, Artemis.* NASA. https://www.nasa.gov/humans-in-space/artemis/.

Spitz, R. (2022–2024). *The Definitive Guide to Thriving on Disruption: Thriving on Disruption* (Vols. 1–4). Disruptive Futures Institute. https://www.thrivingondisruption.com/.

Spitz, R. (2024). *Disrupt with impact: Achieve business success in an unpredictable world.* Kogan Page.

Spitz, R., & Zuin, L. (2020, October 22). How science fiction can help chart your company's path forward when reality flips upside down, SF can accelerate innovation. *Inc.com.* https://www.inc.com/roger-spitz-lidia-zuin/ how-science-fiction-can-accelerate-innovation-foryour-company.html.

Tavis, A., & Lupushor, S. (2022). *Humans at work: The art and practice of creating the hybrid workplace.* Kogan Page.

Toyota. (2023, August 30). *Lunar Cruiser, Toyota's contribution to space exploration.* Toyota Europe. https://www.toyota-europe.com/news/2023/lunar-cruiser.

Jury, K. (2022, March 29). Well-behaved women seldom make history: Quotes and context for women's history month. *Central Penn College.* https://guides.centralpenn.edu/ blog/Well-Behaved-Women-Seldom-Make-History-Quotes-and-Context-for-Womens-History-Month.

Positive psychology: Resilience skills. (n.d.) University of Pennsylvania. Coursera. https://www.coursera.org/learn/ positive-psychology-resilience.

CHAPTER FOUR BEYOND THE DESK: EXPANDING YOUR HORIZONS

"Growth begins at the edge of your comfort zone. Sometimes, you need to venture into the unknown alone, leaving behind the familiar, to truly expand your horizons and discover new possibilities."

Shelli Brunswick

T rue growth and innovation happen beyond the confines of our desks and routines. While these familiar spaces offer security and control, they can also stifle creativity and limit potential. We invite fresh perspectives, enrich our professional lives, and uncover hidden opportunities by stepping out of these comfort zones. As Michelangelo said, "The greatest danger for most of us is not that our aim is too high and we miss it, but that it is too low, and we reach it." This journey is about breaking free from the known and embracing the unknown for personal fulfillment and extraordinary breakthroughs.

Our routines, though comforting, can become traps. Each day can feel predictable and safe, yet ultimately stifling. Like a stagnant pond, we limit our creativity and growth without new challenges. We miss out on the vitality of stepping into the unknown, tackling difficult tasks, and experiencing new discoveries.

The consequences of staying within our boundaries are significant. The world beyond has untapped possibilities—transformative experiences, projects, and connections. Staying within what we know prevents us from discovering hidden talents that emerge when we're pushed to adapt, solve problems, and rise to new challenges.

While the comfort zone feels safe, it's an illusion. True confidence comes from handling change and uncertainty. By stepping outside, we face fears, build resilience, and enrich our lives with new experiences. Each challenge we overcome strengthens our confidence, making us more willing to take on even greater challenges.

Venturing into the unknown doesn't just unlock creativity and confidence—it opens doors to new opportunities. These unseen possibilities are waiting just beyond the familiar. By embracing uncertainty and taking calculated risks, we unlock our full potential. Let's disrupt ourselves and step into the expansive possibilities that await when we leave our desks behind.

Personal Reflections

Early in my assignment at the Pentagon, I faced a pivotal choice. One evening, the Air Force Association hosted an event celebrating the US Air Force Acquisition workforce. No one from my office wanted to go, and I could have easily gone home like everyone else. However, I saw this as an opportunity to network and learn. As a newcomer, I didn't know many people at the reception, but that didn't stop me from making my way around the room, speaking to those I recognized, and introducing myself to new contacts.

Eventually, I approached my boss's boss's boss, a high-ranking government executive known as a Senior Executive Service (SES) member. A few months earlier, I had volunteered to fill in for his executive officer when he went on vacation. Being an executive officer to a general or SES in the military requires dedication, often involving 12–16-hour days. By volunteering for this demanding role, I demonstrated my commitment and work ethic, making it clear that I was serious about my aspirations.

At the reception, the SES learned that an Air Force representative to members of Congress on Capitol Hill, known as a legislative liaison, would soon be departing his position to take on a new assignment elsewhere. Seizing the moment, the SES turned to me and asked, "Brunswick, how would you like to be a legislative liaison?"

Although he didn't hand me the job, he gave me the opportunity to interview for it. With preparation and mentorship from the outgoing liaison, I aced the interview and secured the role. This opportunity, born from stepping out of my comfort zone, transformed my career and taught me the invaluable lesson of embracing risks and seeking new horizons.

The journey beyond our desks is where actual growth and innovation happen. It might be as simple as making a new contact that changes your life. Stepping out of our comfort zones can lead to extraordinary opportunities and personal development, especially in the rapidly evolving space industry. By stepping into unfamiliar territory, we unlock the doors to innovation, personal fulfillment, and extraordinary opportunities. Embrace the unknown, disrupt yourself, and discover the expansive possibilities that lie beyond the ordinary.

Insights From Global Thought Leaders

"True growth happens when you embrace discomfort, take bold risks, and never stop learning. By continually pushing your boundaries, you can turn the art of the possible into reality."

Monique Morrow

Monique Morrow's career is a story of bold risk-taking, relentless curiosity, and adaptability. Describing herself as an "accidental engineer," Monique initially studied French and history but pivoted to technology due to economic pressures and the advice of a family friend. Her professional journey began in Sunnyvale, California, at Advanced Micro Devices (AMD), where she showcased strong skills in crisis management and leading complex projects. This experience laid the foundation for her later roles at Cisco, where she took on increasingly challenging positions, pushing the boundaries of her comfort zone and expanding her expertise, especially in emerging technologies like blockchain and decentralized identity management.

At Cisco, Monique thrived in environments requiring continuous personal and professional evolution. Her time there reinforced her belief in the importance of stepping into the unknown to foster growth. This mindset led to her transition to a startup community, where she became deeply involved in blockchain technology, highlighting her commitment to innovation and exploring new frontiers.

Throughout her career, Monique has embraced the ethos of bold risk-taking. Whether making critical decisions at AMD or pioneering new technologies, she consistently moved beyond her comfort zone, demonstrating that extraordinary results come from venturing into uncharted territories. Her career path underscores the value of seeking challenges—whether by relocating internationally or taking on leadership roles in volatile situations—to achieve substantial growth.

A strong advocate for lifelong learning, Monique's shift from traditional business networking to cutting-edge blockchain applications underscores her dedication to staying ahead of industry trends. She firmly believes in disrupting oneself to avoid being overtaken by rapid technological changes, a proactive approach that has kept her at the forefront of innovation.

Monique's diverse background in both academia and business has been central to her success. She has crafted innovative solutions that challenge conventional thinking by drawing on knowledge across multiple disciplines. Her career exemplifies the power of interdisciplinary approaches and the value of continuous self-reinvention.

Her motto, "Disrupt yourself, or you will be disrupted," captures her proactive philosophy, emphasizing the need for leaders to embrace discomfort and pursue innovation. Monique's human-centric approach to technology ensures that her innovations push boundaries and contribute positively to society. She advocates for fostering environments that promote disruptive thinking and diverse perspectives, essential for nurturing the next generation of innovators.

Monique's journey is a testament to the power of resilience and adaptability in achieving lasting impact in any field. Let it inspire you to embrace learning, take risks, and seek new challenges.

> **"In the heat of challenges, the true strength of a leader is shown not from behind a desk but from the front lines. There, with your team, in the thick of it all, is where real battles are fought and won."**
>
> Bryan Talebi

Bryan Talebi's journey to becoming the CEO and co-founder of Ahura AI is a testament to resilience, vision, and leading from the front. Born in a tiny village in Southeastern Iran, Bryan's early life was marked by significant hardships. His family had to flee Iran due to political persecution, escaping to Turkey and living in a refugee camp before finally gaining asylum in the United States. This early adversity instilled in Bryan a relentless drive to positively impact the world.

Despite the challenges, Bryan showed an early aptitude for education and technology. He taught himself quantum mechanics and differential equations while still in middle school and started working at NASA Goddard Space Flight Center at 16 years old. This remarkable achievement was just the beginning of Bryan's journey in the tech industry.

Bryan's entrepreneurial spirit led him to start his first company while in college, selling educational products to families in underprivileged areas of the United States. This venture taught him valuable lessons about business and the importance of education. He went on to work in several tech startups, helping them achieve significant growth and success.

However, Bryan realized that the education sector had not seen transformative changes for centuries. This realization led him to found Ahura AI, with the vision of using artificial intelligence to revolutionize education and provide personalized learning experiences to millions worldwide. Ahura AI aims to enable people to learn 3 to 5 times faster than traditional education methods, focusing on retraining the workforce for the future job market.

Bryan's leadership style is characterized by leading from the front. He believes in being hands-on and demonstrating the work ethic he expects from his team. During difficult times, Bryan lived on friends' couches. He worked tirelessly to keep Ahura AI afloat, showing his team that he was willing to make personal sacrifices for the company's success.

Bryan's insights on leadership emphasize the importance of being actively involved with your team and surrounding yourself with the right people. He believes that having the right team and mentors is crucial for success. His mentors have provided him with invaluable guidance, especially during challenging times. Bryan's approach to mentorship includes seeking advice only from those who have successfully navigated similar challenges.

Bryan's journey also highlights the importance of embracing discomfort and taking bold risks. His move from Iran to the United States, his early career at NASA, and his ventures into various tech startups were all marked by stepping into unfamiliar territories. Each of these experiences, though challenging, provided him with invaluable lessons and growth opportunities.

Bryan's story encourages professionals to embrace discomfort, take risks, surround themselves with inspiring people, and lead from the front. His journey is not just about personal success but also about making a global impact. He believes education is the key to solving many of the world's challenges. By providing access to quality education, Bryan aims to unlock the intellectual potential of people around the world, enabling them to solve complex problems and create a better future.

Bryan's vision for Ahura AI and his dedication to using technology for social good make him a true leader and innovator in education technology. His story inspires all who seek to make a difference in the world through innovation and leadership.

"Taking action is often the hardest part. Many people have great ideas and visions, but the real challenge lies in turning those visions into reality. However, unless you start doing something, you will never know how many difficulties you will face, how much inspiration you will receive, and how many amazing people you will meet along the way."

Ke Wang

Ke Wang's career exemplifies how growth begins at the edge of one's comfort zone. Initially focused on international law and business, her career path seemed far removed from the world of space exploration. However, her curiosity and willingness to embrace new challenges led her into the innovative frontiers of the space industry.

Ke's transformative journey into space began unexpectedly during her business studies in Europe, where a seemingly ordinary class took an unexpected turn. One day, her professor introduced three young entrepreneurs working in the space sector, a field Ke had barely encountered before. The passion and vision of these young space pioneers captivated her, and the mention of SpaceX ignited a spark. For the first time, she realized that the space industry was evolving beyond government-led initiatives into a new commercial frontier where entrepreneurs and private companies could play a pivotal role.

Intrigued by this fresh perspective, Ke immersed herself in research, discovering that space was no longer an inaccessible field for those without a technical background. Seeing an opportunity to leverage her expertise in law and business, she approached one of the entrepreneurs after class, expressing her desire to learn more and potentially contribute to their efforts. This proactive step led to her becoming CEO of Digital Space, where she organized significant events like the European Commercial Space Summit, partnering with organizations such as the European Space Agency and Airbus to bridge corporate and startup interests in the burgeoning "new space" industry. These experiences taught Ke that in this field, actions spoke louder than ideas.

Through her early steps in the space industry, Ke learned the value of pushing boundaries and taking risks, realizing that determination and a willingness to act were as crucial as any technical expertise. Her journey epitomizes the transformative power of embracing the unknown, as she continuously expanded her horizons by aligning her skills with her newfound passion for space.

Ke's leadership style, grounded in global perspectives and effective communication, has been pivotal in her numerous roles. She fosters collaboration across diverse cultural and professional backgrounds, making her a dynamic mentor. Her openness to learning and adapting has enriched her capabilities and broadened her impact in the industry.

Ke, a co-founder of The Karman Project Foundation, has played a critical role in promoting international and cross-industry collaboration in space. The Foundation aims to break down traditional barriers by fostering trust and cooperation among global leaders in technology, science, business, and the arts. The Karman Project's fellowship program encourages mid-career professionals to bring diverse expertise to the space industry, fostering innovation and a rich exchange of ideas.

Ke also founded the Timenschen Fund with a vision to support ventures focused on applying space technology in unexpected and transformative ways. For Ke, the true potential of space innovation lies in stepping beyond conventional uses and exploring how these technologies can address challenges on Earth, from environmental monitoring to advancing global communications. By investing in pioneering projects that bridge space and everyday life, Ke hopes to inspire a new generation of entrepreneurs to view space as a resource for innovative solutions that expand horizons for all.

Aligned with the Timenschen vision, Ke also founded the Timenschen Institute in 2024 with the goal of growing the space ecosystems in the Middle East and North African (MENA) region. With its flagship programs in education, R&D, and cultural exchange between the MENA countries and the other space-faring nations, Ke is taking her space journey into a new geography on Earth but serving the same purpose of the unity of space.

Her journey from law and business to becoming a leader in space innovation is a testament to the power of stepping outside one's comfort zone and taking bold action. Ke's action-oriented leadership and ability to bridge gaps between the space and non-space sectors have inspired others to explore limitless opportunities in space and beyond.

Ke's story reminds us that leadership is defined by ideas and the actions taken to realize them. As the space industry evolves, she ensures that exploration remains open to diverse professionals eager to contribute to its growth. Her journey encourages lifelong learning, risk-taking, and seeking growth opportunities beyond the familiar—demonstrating that the path beyond the comfort zone is where true innovation flourishes.

Transforming Insights Into Action

True transformation begins when we dare to expand our horizons. By moving beyond the comfort of our routines, we open ourselves to new experiences and perspectives, each one a gateway to greater growth. Embracing the unknown challenges us to adapt, explore, and ultimately discover the full breadth of our potential. Expanding our horizons is about welcoming the unfamiliar, where opportunities for innovation, resilience, and personal fulfillment await.

The first step to growth is to **disrupt yourself**. Continuously seeking new knowledge and skills keeps you competitive and innovative. Growth doesn't happen in comfort; it occurs when you explore unfamiliar territories and expand your horizons. For instance, in *Connecting the Dots: Lessons for Leadership in a Startup World*, John Chambers highlights the importance of constantly evolving and staying ahead in dynamic environments.

Effective leadership starts with action. To **lead from the**

front, you must demonstrate the same work ethic and commitment you expect from others. Being actively involved builds trust and leads to collective success. Steve Harvey emphasizes this in his talk, *Get Out of Your Comfort Zone,* urging leaders to challenge themselves and their teams to exceed expectations.

Cultivating a **growth mindset** means viewing challenges as opportunities for growth rather than obstacles. This mindset is crucial in a constantly changing world, as it empowers us to adapt and thrive in new situations. Stepping outside your comfort zone—where true growth happens—is a foundational element. Instead of simply avoiding discomfort, approach each challenge as a learning experience.

Start with small steps: try something unfamiliar, ask questions, seek feedback, and set goals that require you to stretch. Gradually expanding your comfort zone builds resilience and opens you to experiences that deepen your capabilities. A growth mindset isn't about immediate transformation; it is about embracing continuous learning and making room for failure as part of the journey. Andy Molinsky, in *If You're Not Outside Your Comfort Zone, You Won't Learn Anything,* offers insights into how stepping outside your comfort zone is the key to unlocking new experiences and growth.

Learning from cross-industry experiences is another critical element of growth. Expanding your horizons by drawing lessons from various sectors often leads to breakthroughs and fresh ideas. One important insight from Christie Hunter Arscott's article *Why Women Should Make Bold Moves Early in Their Careers* is to avoid the misconception that risk-taking has only two outcomes: success or failure. Approaching risks with a broader mindset can transform them into growth opportunities. Instead of viewing challenges in terms of "winning or losing," think of each risk as a step toward growth. Whether you achieve your goal or learn something valuable, you are moving forward. To cultivate this mindset, start by exploring unfamiliar environments, industries, or roles that stretch your capabilities. By seeing risks as gateways to learning and innovation, you will build resilience and adaptability, positioning yourself for impactful leadership across any industry.

To stay ahead, it's important to engage in **active participation**. Get involved in industry events, workshops, and volunteer opportunities. Connecting with others and gaining firsthand experience will keep you informed and prepared for emerging trends. Rebecca Patterson's piece *How to Step Out of Your Comfort Zone and Achieve the Impossible* discusses the importance of staying engaged and actively participating in new challenges to foster personal growth.

To transform these insights into action, immerse yourself in professional communities that align with your career goals and aspirations. For those in the space industry, organizations like the Space Generation Advisory Council or the International Astronautical Federation provide invaluable access to industry trends and networks.

If you want to broaden your horizons beyond your field, consider joining organizations supporting your specific professional objectives. For instance, the Project Management Institute is ideal for program managers, while the National Association of Corporate Directors (NACD) offers resources and networking opportunities for individuals pursuing board roles. Leadership-focused groups, such as the International Women's Forum, also provide conferences and programs that unite professionals across sectors. Additionally, attending conferences like the International Astronautical Congress— or others tailored to your field—can offer unique learning opportunities and meaningful connections to help propel your career forward.

Volunteering your skills to organizations is a powerful way to gain hands-on experience, contribute to a meaningful cause, and build relationships with professionals and leaders. For those in the space sector, organizations like the Space

Court Foundation or the World Space Week Association offer opportunities to engage deeply with industry challenges. Outside the space industry, consider volunteering with groups that align with your interests and expertise, such as Habitat for Humanity, which brings together people across professions to support affordable housing projects, or Women in Aerospace, which empowers women and young people interested in aerospace and aviation.

Other organizations like the American Red Cross provide volunteer opportunities for those interested in crisis management and healthcare, while the Junior Achievement program offers professionals the chance to mentor students in entrepreneurship and financial literacy. Bryan Talebi illustrates this idea of hands-on involvement in *Simulation Podcast #452, Bryan Talebi: AI & Education*, where he emphasizes the importance of learning through action and engagement. Volunteering allows you to gain valuable insights, expand your network, and make a positive impact, regardless of your industry.

Continuous learning is essential for staying competitive in an ever-changing world. Developing expertise in areas both within and beyond your field not only builds adaptability but can also lead to unexpected breakthroughs. Pursue courses, certifications, or books in emerging fields to stay ahead —whether it is gaining insight into negotiation techniques through *Never Split the Difference* by Chris Voss or exploring advancements in quantum computing with *Quantum Supremacy* by Michio Kaku. Stories like those in *Hidden Figures*, where pioneering Black women at NASA achieved groundbreaking results through relentless learning and persistence, show that expanding knowledge across disciplines can lead to remarkable success, even in challenging environments.

Seeking **mentorship** and leadership roles is essential for personal and professional growth. To find a mentor, start by identifying individuals whose career paths or skills align with your goals. Professional organizations, industry events, and networking platforms like LinkedIn can be great places to connect with potential mentors. Approach them with a thoughtful message, expressing genuine interest in their work and explaining how you believe their guidance could support your development.

Taking on projects that challenge you will also help you make the most of mentorship, allowing you to gain real insights as you navigate new territory. *The Right Stuff*, a film about the first astronauts in the Project Mercury program, illustrates the impact of mentorship and leadership in high-stakes environments, highlighting how both are key drivers of resilience and success.

Now is the time to take that bold step into your personal "uncharted cosmos." Whether it is pursuing a new professional endeavor, overcoming a personal fear, or diving into a new hobby, every significant achievement starts with the courage to venture into the unknown. **Engage actively with communities**, develop your leadership skills through workshops, and take concrete actions toward goals that stretch your boundaries. Reflect on your experiences, adjust your approach, and keep moving forward.

Stepping out from behind your desk is not just about career advancement—it's a path to personal transformation. You unlock creativity, confidence, and growth by embracing new experiences, challenging limitations, and pushing boundaries. Growth doesn't come from routine; it comes from exploration. Bold exploration yields the most profound discoveries and deepest fulfillment. Elizabeth Gilbert touches on this idea in her TED Talk, *Your Elusive Creative Genius,* where she speaks about embracing the unknown to unlock creative potential. Embrace the unknown, trust in your ability to adapt, and let your journey into new territories lead you to extraordinary opportunities.

Resources

Arscott, C. H. (2022, July 6). Why women should make bold moves early in their careers. *Harvard Business Review.* https://hbr.org/2022/07/why-women-should-make-bold-moves-early-in-their-careers.

Chambers, J., & Brady, D. (2018). *Connecting the dots: Lessons for leadership in a startup world.* Hachette Books.

Harvey, S. (2018, October 9). *Get out of your comfort zone* [Video]. YouTube. https://www.youtube.com/watch?v=WYR-gxVcg6s.

Hidden Figures [Film]. (2016). 20th Century Studios.

Kaku, M. (2023.) *Quantum supremacy: How the quantum computer revolution will change everything.* Vintage.

Kaufman, P. (Director). (1983). *The right stuff* [Film]. Warner Brothers.

McConaughey, M. (2023, November 12). *5 minutes for the next 50yYears—Matthew McConaughey motivational speech* [Video]. YouTube. https://www.youtube.com/watch?v=QbL0X3B4mjg.

Michelangelo Quotes. (n.d.) BrainyQuote.com. Retrieved September 20, 2024, from https://www.brainyquote.com/quotes/michelangelo_108779.

Molinsky, A. (2016, July 29). If you're not outside your comfort zone, You won't learn anything. *Harvard Business Review.* https://hbr.org/2016/07/if-youre-not-outside-your-comfort-zone-you-wont-learn-anything.

Patterson, R. (2020, June 10). How to step out of your comfort zone and achieve the "impossible." *Forbes.* https://www.forbes.com/councils/forbescoachescouncil/2020/06/10/how-to-step-out-of-your-comfort-zone-and-achieve-the-impossible/.

Talebi, B. (Host). (2019, June 27). AI & education (No. 452) [Video & audio podcast episode on YouTube]. In *Simulation Podcast.* https://www.youtube.com/watch?v=Z_nmqkEFR0w.

Voss, C. (2016). *Never split the difference: Negotiating as if your life depended on it.* Harper Business.

CHAPTER FIVE ORBITING CONNECTIONS: THE SIGNIFICANCE OF RELATIONSHIPS

"Time is the canvas on which we paint our relationships; be intentional with your strokes. Understanding each other's perspectives enriches the hues, and making time for those who matter turns fleeting moments into lasting memories."

Shelli Brunswick

H umans are inherently social creatures, and our need for connection, belonging, and support is fundamental to our well-being, growth, and achievement. Relationships are the foundation for success in the vast expanse of the space industry, where collaboration and teamwork are paramount. During my over-35-year career, I've learned that the essence of life in any field is deeply rooted in the connections we cultivate. Whether in aerospace, business, or daily life, our relationships shape our journey and ultimately determine our success.

Success is not just about the knowledge or skills we acquire; it is also about our ability to build and maintain relationships with colleagues, customers, and partners. These connections create a resilient support network that can weather challenges, unlock new possibilities, and inspire us to reach greater heights. This principle extends beyond the space industry—collaboration and teamwork are essential to success.

Drawing on insights from global thought leaders and my personal experiences, I will explore the transformative impact of meaningful connections and professional relationships.

From early family mentors to expansive global networks, the relationships you nurture influence your course, drive your advancement, and are the threads that weave strength, resilience, and opportunity into the tapestry of your life.

Building a strong network is more than just exchanging business cards—it is about forming genuine connections with individuals who share your vision and values. These relationships, founded on trust, respect, and open communication, are the essential pillars of any strong connection. Think of your network as a web, where each connection strengthens the whole, transforming it into a powerful tool for growth. A robust network acts both as a safety net and a springboard, linking you with those who can guide you, support your ambitions, and introduce you to new opportunities.

Networking in the community, industry, and professional organizations must be purposeful and authentic. You should actively engage in industry events, leverage platforms like LinkedIn, and participate in discussions that resonate with your goals. Follow up with new contacts and maintain these relationships by offering continuous value and support.

Effective networking does not just boost your visibility; it also builds confidence and opens the door to diverse opportunities. By joining professional associations or community groups, you not only gain access to exclusive resources but also find a sense of belonging and opportunities for growth.

WomenTech Network hosted an International Women's Day event that provided a particularly inspiring example of the power of networking. I had the privilege of moderating a panel featuring leading women in the space industry, including a space lawyer from Africa. Her story of overcoming significant challenges resonated deeply with a young woman from Namibia, who attended the event virtually.

Due to socioeconomic and cultural barriers in her country, people frequently told this young woman that her dream of becoming a space lawyer was impossible. Seeing someone with a similar background who had succeeded in the space industry gave her the courage to pursue her dreams. After the event, she reached out to me, expressing how deeply inspired she was and how the panelist's journey had reignited her passion.

I connected her with the space lawyer from the panel, and this initiated a mentoring relationship that provided her with guidance, support, and access to critical resources. Through this mentorship, she was able to further her education, expand her professional network, and begin carving out a path for herself in the space industry. This connection not only transformed her career but also inspired others in her community to pursue their dreams, proving that with the proper support, anything is possible.

Mentorship, much like networking, is a powerful force in career development. It is about the mutual exchange of knowledge and experience that enriches both the mentor and the mentee. Through the WomenTech Network Mentoring Program, I had the privilege of mentoring an individual who had recently relocated to the US with his family.

Facing the challenges of adapting to a new country, culture, and community, he initially felt personally and professionally isolated. Our mentoring relationship provided him with critical guidance—not only to advance in his career, he earned a promotion and completed an executive MBA, but also to help his family find their place in this new environment.

Through our discussions, he gained insights about connecting with his community's local organizations. As a result of these insights, his children joined sports programs, and his family participated in community volunteer activities. This experience illustrates how mentorship can create a ripple effect, empowering the mentee to succeed professionally while also supporting their family's journey to build meaningful connections and a sense of belonging in a new community.

I also grew through this mentoring relationship. I gained new insights into the challenges faced by professionals relocating to a foreign country. It enriched my understanding of global work environments. This experience enhanced my empathy and adaptability, helping me become a more effective leader and mentor. It also kept me attuned to emerging trends and practices across diverse fields, broadening my knowledge and expertise.

In today's digital age, technology enables us to maintain and enhance these relationships across distances. Online platforms like LinkedIn and Zoom provide invaluable ways to connect with mentors from around the world, offering access to expertise that might otherwise be out of reach—particularly for those in highly specialized fields. These tools make it possible for mentorship to remain a vibrant, dynamic part of our professional lives, enabling mentors and mentees to share insights, celebrate achievements, and support each other's growth, regardless of geographic boundaries.

These experiences taught me that the relationships we cultivate—whether through networking or mentorship—are true catalysts for progress. They are the cornerstones of our success, providing the wisdom, support, and inspiration needed to navigate challenges and seize opportunities. As you continue your journey, let professional and mentorship relationships be the foundation upon which you build your individual and collective achievements.

Personal Reflections

From an early age, I learned the value of being a "joiner," a quality deeply instilled by my family. Their unwavering guidance, mentorship, and encouragement taught me the importance of building and nurturing genuine connections. Growing up with remarkable role models like my mother, Aunt Barb, and Grandmother Rose, I developed resilience, perseverance, and an unshakeable belief in what I could achieve.

My mother, a trailblazing executive in the male-dominated manufacturing industry, defied expectations daily, teaching me that no goal was out of reach. Her strength and courage constantly reminded me that I could forge my own path without limits.

My grandmother, an extraordinary entrepreneur, ran a dairy farm and a bar with my grandfather while raising five children. She embodied grit, resourcefulness, and ambition. Her example showed me the power of hard work and self-sufficiency.

My Aunt Barb, an inspiring elementary school teacher, encouraged her young students—and me—to dream big and be bold. She was a steadfast supporter throughout my career, always urging me to reach higher. These incredible women were my first mentors, each leaving an indelible mark on my life, instilling in me the foundations of leadership, determination, and the courage to carve my own path.

My stepfather, Marshall, an accomplished real estate agent, demonstrated the importance of relationships in personal and professional contexts. He used his passion for golf as a leisure activity and networking tool, forging and strengthening relationships on the golf course. His ability to translate personal interests into community success and professional achievements through golf tournaments and social events taught me early on how trust and mutual respect can lead to sustained success.

As I embarked on my career in the United States Air Force (USAF), these foundational lessons vividly came to life. I actively sought out and joined organizations filled with like-minded individuals, such as the Air Force Association (AFA), the National Defense Industrial Association (NDIA), and the Company Grade Officers Association (CGOA). Participating in these groups provided me with opportunities for specialized training, critical mentoring, and insights that were instrumental to my development.

A pivotal moment in my career came when Colonel Keith Zuegel hired me as a USAF Legislative Liaison to the US House of Representatives. On my first day, he shared a piece of wisdom that resonated deeply: "Life is all about relationships." This advice reinforced my experiences growing up and shaped my professional interactions and strategies. While working for Colonel Zuegel, I learned the nuances of strategic relationships and their critical role in leadership and policy development.

As my career progressed and my roles evolved, so did my affiliations and networks. I transitioned to organizations that matched my growing focus on global leadership and empowerment, such as Women in Aerospace, the World Business Angels Investment Forum, the G100, and the Space4Women Mentoring Program of the United Nations Office of Outer Space Affairs (UNOOSA). These affiliations brought new challenges and learning opportunities, further expanding my worldview and professional network.

Throughout my career, I've attended and spoken at various conferences, including the AFA's Air and Space Conference, the Space Congress, the Space Symposium, and international events like the International Astronautical Congress (IAC) and the European Rover Challenge: Humans2Mars Summit European Edition. These platforms enhanced my knowledge and exposure and allowed me to contribute to broader discussions on space innovation, leadership, and technology.

Reflecting on my journey, I cannot overstate the importance of the relationships I've built. These connections have provided support, resources, and inspiration, enabling me to overcome challenges and seize opportunities. The wisdom imparted by my parents, mentors, and leaders like Colonel Zuegel has been instrumental in shaping my path and approach to life.

My journey underscores that nurturing solid and meaningful relationships is crucial to personal and professional growth. As my career evolves, the relationships built on trust and mutual respect remain the bedrock of my success.

Insights From Global Thought Leaders

"Networking is not just about connecting; it's about integrating —immersively, inclusively, and intentionally—with the cultures and communities that shape our professional landscapes. Each relationship we forge is a bridge to a new horizon, a lesson in leadership, and a step

towards global understanding."

Andrea Prazakova

Andrea Prazakova's journey from the Czech Republic to becoming a global banking executive highlights the profound impact of genuine leadership and the power of nurturing relationships across cultures. From a young age, Andrea, raised in an environment that empowered and actively engaged women in all spheres of life, developed a strong sense of resilience and her own abilities. Her father instilled in her the importance of perseverance and courage, teaching her to face challenges head-on without yielding to setbacks.

One of the most defining moments in Andrea's career happened early on when she encountered a major setback in her first banking role. As a young professional, she stepped into a demanding environment, eager yet unprepared for the intense challenges that came her way. The weight of expectations and her own inexperience left her questioning if she was truly cut out for the job. Feeling overwhelmed and close to giving up, Andrea confided in her father, who had always been a guiding presence in her life. A former professional hockey player and coach, he had faced his own share of setbacks, and he understood the resilience it took to keep moving forward. Instead of letting her quit, he reminded her that real growth often comes from pushing through difficult moments. His words encouraged her to dig deep, stay the course, and confront the challenges head-on.

Choosing to persevere, Andrea found her footing and grew to meet the role's demands and excel beyond them. Her father's advice became a cornerstone in her life, teaching her that setbacks are launching pads to greater strength and resilience. This early lesson shaped her approach to every challenge that followed, transforming obstacles into opportunities and instilling in her confidence that she could overcome any trial on her path.

Andrea's career journey is a testament to her courage in

seizing unexpected opportunities and embracing new paths. While working as a waitress in the Czech Republic, her life took a transformative turn after the fall of communism. A friend mentioned that an Austrian bank was seeking German-speaking talent to support its expanding operations in newly opened markets. Although Andrea had no experience in banking and had not yet relocated, she saw this as a rare opportunity to redefine her future. Driven by determination, she applied, was hired, and soon made the bold move to Austria. This transition proved pivotal; her linguistic skills, insatiable curiosity, and adaptability propelled her quickly through the ranks. This single courageous step laid the foundation for a remarkable 32-year career, taking her across continents—from Europe to Asia, Africa, and the Middle East—broadening her understanding of diverse cultures and business practices, and shaping her into a versatile and respected global leader.

A key aspect of Andrea's leadership style is her commitment to authentic team engagement. By working alongside her team—counting cash as a teller or participating in daily customer service tasks—Andrea demonstrated her dedication to understanding the on-ground realities of banking operations. This hands-on approach earned her genuine respect and loyalty from her employees, who saw her commitment to supporting them in their daily challenges. Her leadership approach fostered a culture of mutual respect and collaboration and even contributed to the team winning a branch performance competition, recognizing their excellence in service and operations.

Her belief in transformational rather than transactional relationships further enhanced Andrea's ability to connect with her teams on a personal level. She focused on building bridges between different cultures and professional practices, emphasizing the human aspect of business interactions. Her leadership fostered an environment where diverse teams felt valued and understood, which was crucial in her role overseeing retail banking operations across Africa.

Reflecting on her leadership philosophy, Andrea often says, "True leadership is about making genuine connections with your people. It's about showing up as a leader and a team member willing to share in the day-to-day challenges." Andrea's career is a testament to the effectiveness of authentic leadership and the importance of resilience. Her ability to seamlessly integrate into various cultural settings, her hands-on approach, and her commitment to empathetic leadership have left a lasting impact on her teams and the broader banking industry. Her journey underscores the significance of building deep, meaningful connections and the enduring value of perseverance and adaptability in facing challenges.

Andrea's journey highlights the importance of building networks, cultural awareness, mentorship, and, most importantly, curiosity, which she says is her superpower. She stresses the importance of integrating oneself into new cultural contexts. She built strong relationships, created meaningful products and experiences, stood out with high-quality work, cultivated cultural sensitivity, and fostered inclusive environments. Andrea valued mentorship and coaching, recognizing that informal guidance from colleagues, superiors, and family could significantly shape one's career.

Effectively managing stakeholders required active engagement and understanding of their perspectives, which was critical when leading diverse teams across different regions. Above all, her father's lessons on persistence taught her the importance of sticking it out and pushing through challenges, reinforcing that resilience and determination are essential for success.

Andrea's story is a powerful example of how authentic leadership, cultural awareness, and perseverance can shape a successful career and build solid and impactful relationships across the globe. Her insights and experiences provide valuable lessons for anyone looking to navigate their professional journey with integrity and resilience.

"Relationships are the bedrock of any successful venture. They provide the support, resources, and inspiration needed to overcome challenges and seize opportunities."

Arpit Chaturvedi

Arpit Chaturvedi's career highlights several key insights on building networks, promoting mentorship, and leveraging relationships. Born in India, Arpit's curiosity and drive led him to pursue higher education and diverse professional experiences globally. His journey began with a Bachelor of Arts in History from Kirori Mal College at the University of Delhi, followed by an MBA in Human Resource Management from the Symbiosis Centre for Management and Human Resource Development. His Master of Public Administration (MPA) from Cornell University significantly shaped his perspective on global governance, policy, and sustainability.

At Cornell, Arpit was the first non-US citizen to be Editor-in-Chief of the Cornell Policy Review. This pivotal role allowed him to network with influential academics and professionals and laid the groundwork for his future endeavors. His tenure at Cornell also underscored the importance of mentorship, as professors and peers provided guidance and opened doors to numerous opportunities.

Arpit's natural talent for bringing people together to create value became apparent early in his college years. During his undergraduate studies, he established debating societies that served as platforms for vibrant discussions and intellectual exchange. This passion for fostering collaboration carried into his professional life, where he later built networks that connected like-minded professionals across various sectors. His role as a legislative assistant to a Member of Parliament in India further sharpened his skills in public policy and advocacy. Through this experience, Arpit recognized the profound need for knowledge-sharing platforms that promote dialogue on critical issues, including sustainability and diplomacy.

His journey took him to San Francisco State University,

where he taught a graduate-level course on Comparative Perspectives in Public Administration. This experience reinforced his belief in the importance of diverse perspectives and global learning. Upon returning to India, Arpit was instrumental in setting up the Indian School of Public Policy in New Delhi, aiming to balance global perspectives and local needs.

Arpit's creation of the Global Policy, Diplomacy, and Sustainability (GPODS) Fellowship is a testament to his vision and dedication. Recognizing the limitations of traditional academic settings, he co-founded GPODS to bridge the gap between academic knowledge and practical skills. The fellowship program provides a platform for public policy practitioners, business professionals, energy and climate change experts, entrepreneurs, academicians, scholars, and strategic analysts to build a foundational understanding of global governance, policy, sustainable ecosystems, and strategic issues.

Arpit's global experiences have taught him the importance of understanding and integrating into diverse cultural contexts, which is crucial for building strong, effective relationships. He believes in the power of standing out by consistently delivering high-quality work and fostering inclusive environments. Arpit's proactive approach to networking has always been about adding value and being culturally sensitive.

Arpit benefited from informal mentorship throughout his journey, receiving support and guidance from colleagues and superiors. According to Arpit, "mentorship not only provides guidance but also builds confidence and resilience." Effective stakeholder management involves understanding their perspectives and building strong relationships. Arpit's ability to engage with diverse stakeholders has been critical in his career.

Arpit's journey and his insights on networking and mentorship provide valuable lessons for anyone looking to make a meaningful impact in their field. His creation of the GPODS Fellowship is a testament to his vision of fostering global leadership and creating access points for professionals to drive meaningful change. Through his experiences, Arpit demonstrates that building solid relationships, being culturally aware, and embracing mentorship are critical to career success.

"I learned to appreciate the value of networking. A substantial majority of my pursuits have been fostered by my good relationships with like-minded individuals in the industry, and it further encouraged me to give back to those wishing to start their journey."

Ruvimbo Samanga

Ruvimbo Samanga's journey into the space industry is a compelling story of resilience, ambition, and strategic relationship-building. Originally from Bulawayo, Zimbabwe, she faced numerous crossroads before finding her path in space law. During her second-to-last year of undergraduate studies, Ruvimbo was unsure of her career direction, having explored various fields without finding one that truly resonated. She describes this period as overwhelming, with countless potential directions but no clear calling. However, her innate curiosity and boldness to step beyond her comfort zone led her to the Manfred Lachs Space Law Moot Court competition. This venture seemed almost improbable, given her limited exposure to space law. Driven by the challenge, she dove headfirst into understanding the intricacies of space law, an experience that would not only ignite her passion for the field but redefine her career. Her success in the competition ignited a love for space law, and she returned the following year as the coach of the team, leading them to a historic victory as the first African team to win the competition in its 26-year history. This journey transformed her perspective and set her on an inspiring path within the space industry.

Ruvimbo's success is also a testament to the power of networking and mentorship. She credits much of her progress to the invaluable guidance of mentors like Professor Timiebi Aganaba-Jeanty, a respected space law expert who not only offered advice but actively created opportunities for her to thrive. Early in Ruvimbo's journey, Professor Aganaba-Jeanty encouraged her participation in initiatives that broadened her understanding of space law's global impact and expanded her network. These programs and relationships have been pivotal to Ruvimbo's growth, enabling her to make meaningful contributions to the development of space law in Africa and advocate for greater inclusion in the industry.

Early in her career, Ruvimbo learned the importance of building a network of like-minded individuals who shared her passion for space and development. Her involvement with organizations like the Space Generation Advisory Council (SGAC) provided her with platforms to engage with global leaders, attend international conferences, and contribute to policy discussions. These experiences were instrumental in expanding her network and deepening her understanding of the global space economy.

Ruvimbo believes that effective networking is not about amassing numerous business cards but about forming genuine connections that can lead to collaborative opportunities. Her ability to connect with others personally has been pivotal in her career. Whether through professional engagements or informal conversations, Ruvimbo emphasizes the importance of being authentic and showing genuine interest in the people she meets. Her strategic approach to networking has allowed her to collaborate with global leaders and gain valuable insights, further enhancing her ability to make a significant impact in the space industry.

Ruvimbo is also deeply committed to mentoring the next generation of space professionals. She believes in the importance of giving back and supporting those who are just starting their journeys. Her various initiatives and collaborations reflect her efforts to foster a supportive and inclusive community within the space sector. Mentorship has played a significant role in Ruvimbo's journey. She attributes much of her success to the guidance and support she received from mentors who were generous with their knowledge and time. These mentors provided her with invaluable insights into navigating the complexities of the space industry and encouraged her to pursue her dreams despite the challenges.

Ruvimbo also values lifelong learning. She continues to look for opportunities for professional development and is committed to giving back by mentoring young professionals in the space industry. Empathy and a desire to uplift others underpin her approach to mentorship, reflecting the support she received during her career.

Ruvimbo's journey was not without its challenges. She faced significant socioeconomic and technical hurdles that often seemed insurmountable, particularly given the limited resources available for space law in her home country. Early on, Ruvimbo experienced self-doubt, questioning whether she belonged in the space industry—a field often perceived as accessible only to those with extensive resources and elite connections. Despite these internal struggles, her passion for space law and commitment to advocating for marginalized communities drove her to persevere. She recalls moments of uncertainty, especially during her participation in the Manfred Lachs Space Law Moot Court competition, when the weight of competing on an international stage felt overwhelming. Yet, each small victory and the support of mentors strengthened her resolve. Ruvimbo's ability to confront self-doubt and persist through adversity became a defining aspect of her journey, fueling her achievements and her dedication to promoting reforms that uplift vulnerable communities.

Her involvement with various organizations has provided platforms to advance her career and contribute to the broader space community. She is active with the SGAC. From 2019 to 2021, she served as Zimbabwe's National Point of Contact on the Advisory Council for SGAC. She also received recognition as the best participant in the inaugural cohort of the African Space Leadership Institute's (ASLI) African Space Policy Course. This organization offers valuable opportunities for professionals and students interested in space science and policy to connect, learn, and collaborate. She has since been recognized as a Young Space Leader by the International Astronautical Federation and, in 2024, received the Young Achiever Award from the International Institute of Space Law.

Ruvimbo's journey exemplifies the significance of building strong, authentic relationships, effective networking, and the transformative power of mentorship. Ruvimbo's story serves as a beacon for aspiring professionals in the space industry, showcasing how resilience, strategic networking, and effective mentorship can overcome significant barriers. Through her dedication and vision, Ruvimbo continues to inspire and empower the next generation of space leaders.

Transforming Insights Into Action

Building strong, supportive relationships is essential for both personal and professional success. These connections provide guidance and support and open doors to new opportunities. **Mentorship** is a crucial part of this process. It's essential to seek out mentors who can offer valuable insights while being open to mentoring others in return. This mutual exchange of knowledge fosters growth for everyone involved, as highlighted in *Never Eat Alone* by Keith Ferrazzi, which emphasizes the power of building authentic relationships to achieve success.

Engaging with **professional organizations** and attending events can significantly expand your network. Connecting with a diverse range of people from various industries, cultures, and perspectives enriches your understanding and promotes innovation. Erin Meyer explores this idea in *The Culture Map*, illustrating how cross-cultural communication can enhance collaboration and problem-solving. Additionally, articles like *A Beginner's Guide to Networking* from Harvard Business Review offer practical strategies for building and maintaining relationships. One approach I find particularly valuable is building connections at all levels.

Connecting with peers is essential, but forming relationships with individuals at various levels across and outside your organization is equally important. For example, reaching out to your manager's peers or even your boss's boss can lead to new perspectives and open doors to growth opportunities. In her article *Why Managing Up to Your Boss Is Not Enough*, Jenny Wood explains, "When people of influence know you, they can advocate for you, offer you high-profile projects, and support your career goals." By cultivating relationships across different levels, you strengthen your network and gain advocates who can champion your professional advancement.

When you form **genuine connections**, you open yourself up to new perspectives and collaborative opportunities. Deep and authentic relationships make your network valuable: it is about quality over quantity. For those who may feel shy or anxious about networking, start with small, manageable steps to develop this skill. Begin by preparing thoughtful questions or compliments, as Dale Carnegie suggests in *How to Win Friends and Influence People*, to make a positive impression. For example, at a networking event, you could start by complimenting someone's presentation or asking about a topic you know they are passionate about. Another approach is to engage one-on-one or in smaller groups, which can feel less overwhelming than large gatherings. Set simple goals, like connecting with one new person per event or following up with an existing contact every few weeks. Over time, practicing these steps helps build confidence and gradually expands your network with meaningful connections.

Collaboration is key to achieving shared goals and overcoming challenges that are difficult to tackle alone. Working together allows you to combine strengths and resources. In his book, *The Law of Success,* Napoleon Hill calls this the "Master Mind" concept. In other words, it refers to utilizing a group of minds to accomplish individual or shared goals. In difficult times, your network can provide the support you need to persevere, as discussed in *Innovation Lessons from Dad: The Super Connector*, an article in Forbes Technology Council that emphasizes the role of strong relationships in innovation and resilience.

Regularly **assessing your relationships** ensures they align with your long-term goals. Setting objectives to expand or deepen connections where necessary helps build a network that supports your aspirations. In today's digital world, **technology** plays a crucial role in maintaining relationships, especially over distances. Webinars and virtual networking events offer opportunities to connect with professionals across industries. For example, WomenTech Network hosts various virtual conferences and events, including their annual conference, which brings together women in tech, minorities, and allies from around the globe. This interactive platform offers live educational and training content, keynotes, engaging panels, breakout rooms, technical workshops, and networking opportunities through both virtual and in-person sessions. One example of the networking opportunities available through WomenTech Network is the webinar *Space For All: Women in Spacetech & How You Can Be One Too*, which I have had the pleasure of participating in.

To find events tailored to your field, platforms like Eventbrite, LinkedIn, and professional organization websites are excellent resources. Search terms like "[your industry] webinars" or "virtual networking for [your profession]." For instance, someone in marketing could search "marketing webinars," while those in healthcare might try "virtual networking for healthcare professionals." This approach can work across any industry, from engineering to education, helping uncover events that align with your career interests and provide meaningful connections.

As you take these steps, you will build a robust network supporting your personal and professional growth. **Relationships are the cornerstone of success**. Nurturing them with sincerity and purpose will lead to extraordinary achievements. In our interconnected world, no great accomplishment is achieved alone. Collaboration, shared knowledge, and mutual support are the keys to transforming challenges into opportunities.

To further strengthen your journey, consider engaging with **professional organizations** such as the AFA, the Space Generation Advisory Council (SGAC), and Women in Aerospace (WIA). These organizations provide networking, professional development, and platforms for collaboration across industries. Conferences like the International Astronautical Congress (IAC) and ASCEND offer additional opportunities to connect with industry leaders and innovators.

Participating in these events and organizations lets you stay informed about the latest advancements and trends while expanding your professional network. Your relationships will shape your career and have a lasting impact on your industry and beyond. The future is bright, and the connections you cultivate today will propel you to new heights, contributing to a world where collective progress and individual success go hand in hand.

References

Brunswick, S. (2023, April 21). Mother's day inspiration: Mentorship should be core to Business culture. *Forbes.* https://www.forbes.com/councils/forbestechcouncil/2023/04/21/mothers-day-inspiration-mentorship-should-be-core-to-business-culture/.

Brunswick, S. (2023, May 23). Innovation lessons from dad: The super connector. *Forbes* https://www.forbes.com/councils/forbestechcouncil/2023/05/23/innovation-lessons-from-dad-the-super-connector/.

Carnegie, D. (1998). *How to win friends and influence people.* Gallery Books.

Ferrazzi, K., & Raz, T. (2005). *Never eat alone and other secrets to success: One relationship at a time.* Currency Doubleday.

Hill, N. (2008). *The law of success: The master wealth-builder's complete and original lesson plan for achieving your dreams.* TarcherPerigee.

Koifman, N. (2023, July 5). The importance of mentorship. *Forbes.* https://www.forbes.com/sites/forbesbusinesscouncil/2023/07/05/the-importance-of-mentorship/.

Meyer, E. (2014). *The culture map: Breaking through the invisible boundaries of global business.* PublicAffairs.

Ravishankar, R. A. (2023, March 22). A beginner's guide to networking. *Harvard Business Review.* https://hbr.org/2023/03/a-beginners-guide-to-networking.

Smanga, R. (2023). Personal correspondence interview. Shelli Brunswick [Interviewer], 20 February; approved 26 August 2024.

WomenTech Network. (2022, Feb 12). *Space for all: Women in spacetech & how you can be one too* [Video]. YouTube. https://www.youtube.com/watch?v=u-gExSftMDs.

WomenTech Network. (2023, Feb 27). *Transformational mentoring: Inspiring global change makers* [Video]. YouTube. https://www.youtube.com/watch?v=qST5A6KXyf8.

Wood, J. (2023). Why managing up to your boss is not enough. *Harvard Business Review.* https://hbr.org/2023/02/why-managing-up-to-your-boss-is-not-enough.

CHAPTER SIX BEYOND SELF-DOUBT: NEVER DISQUALIFY YOURSELF FROM SOMETHING YOU HAVEN'T BEEN OFFERED

"Embrace the unknown and trust in your potential. The opportunities you dare to pursue, even when uncertain, often lead to the most remarkable growth and success."

Shelli Brunswick

Have you ever dreamed of something so bold that it filled you with doubt? Have you heard that insidious little voice that tells you that you are not experienced enough, qualified enough, or are not deserving of it? This voice is imposter syndrome and it lies to us all. It takes immense courage to challenge that voice and say, "I am enough. I am qualified. I deserve this opportunity." This act of courage is not just a declaration; it is a powerful step toward reaching your potential.

Recognizing self-doubt is the first step to overcoming it. By reframing negative thoughts, seeking support, and practicing self-compassion, we begin to unlock our full potential. When you hear that voice of doubt, try to identify the specific negative thought and challenge it with a positive one. Seeking support from friends, family, or a mentor who can provide a different perspective may help you overcome your self-doubts. And remember to be kind to yourself, especially when you're uncertain. As Harriet Tubman said, "Every great dream begins with a dreamer." Her courage and unwavering belief in the possibility of change remind us that no dream is too big when we harness our inner strength.

Yet self-doubt doesn't only come from within. External barriers such as socioeconomic status, access to technology, and societal expectations often amplify self-doubt. These factors can make us feel inadequate, but it's important to remember that overcoming these obstacles is possible through strategic efforts like seeking scholarships, free learning resources, and mentorship. In today's digital age, technical barriers can also hold us back. Promoting digital inclusion and leveraging public resources help to bridge the knowledge gap.

Self-limiting beliefs, often rooted in past experiences, are mental barriers that limit our growth. It's crucial to recognize and challenge these beliefs, replace them with positive self-talk, and practice self-compassion. Treat yourself with kindness, as you would a friend or a child facing self-doubt.

Surround yourself with people who share your values but bring grounded perspectives, and seek mentors whose feedback helps you build a more accurate and empowered self-image. Embracing these challenges becomes more than a task-it is a pathway to a stronger, more authentic self.

External voices can also plant seeds of doubt. Sometimes, our well-intentioned friends and family try to shield us from disappointment, while others might view our ambitions as threatening. Nobel Peace Laureate Desmond Tutu once said, "We are each made for goodness, love, and compassion." Recognizing our worth and surrounding ourselves with people who see our potential creates an environment where self-doubt fades and self-belief flourishes.

Overcoming self-doubt is about silencing the inner critic and turning it into a catalyst for growth. The journey involves cultivating compassion, challenging limiting beliefs, and pursuing every opportunity with courage. Your potential is limitless—don't let self-doubt stand in your way. Embrace your full potential and transform it into a force for success.

Personal Reflections

One of the most valuable lessons I have learned in my career is to never disqualify myself from something I have not been offered. This lesson became especially clear when I decided to retire from the Air Force and was contemplating my next career move. As I began exploring possibilities, I mentioned my retirement to colleagues, asking them to keep me in mind for potential opportunities.

One day, a peer shared a job announcement for the chief operating officer (COO) position at Space Foundation. Initially, I hesitated. The idea of competing against over 170 potentially more qualified candidates was daunting. I even asked my coworkers if I should apply, wondering if I was the right fit. At that moment, my friend and colleague, Vanessa, gave me insightful advice, "Never disqualify yourself from something you haven't been offered."

After hearing Vanessa's words of encouragement, I decided to apply. The process was rigorous, involving several interviews and months of waiting. Each stage brought its own set of challenges and doubts, but I persisted, reminding myself of Vanessa's advice. Eventually, I received the news—I was selected to become the COO.

This experience made me realize how often we exclude ourselves from opportunities before giving ourselves a chance. We create barriers in our minds, limiting our potential for growth and success. Had I not taken that chance, I would have missed out on a role that profoundly shaped my career and set the stage for the rest of my professional life.

So, keep an open mind and never disqualify yourself from an opportunity before it is presented. You never know what doors might open when you dare to take a chance on yourself. By sharing this story, I hope to inspire you to silence your inner critic, take bold steps, and trust in your potential to achieve remarkable growth and success.

Insights From Global Thought Leaders

"Don't listen to the outside voices; listen to the inside voices. They keep you going."

Dr. Vanessa Farsadaki

Dr. Vanessa Farsadaki, known fondly as Dr. V, embodies resilience and innovation in space health, her journey mirroring the allegory of the "determined frog" who scales a seemingly insurmountable mountain despite the doubts and discouragement of others. This story illustrates the power of inner focus and the importance of ignoring negative external influences. This allegory resonates with Dr. V because her path has been shaped by the strength to persist and tune out external doubts. Born in New York but raised across different continents due to her mother's diplomatic assignments, Vanessa grew up adapting to various cultures, learning languages, and honing flexibility that would become indispensable in her pioneering work in AstroMedicine.

Vanessa's academic path was anything but linear. Early hurdles in Switzerland, where strict residency policies blocked her entry into medical school, pushed her to pursue alternate disciplines like biology and genetics. What initially felt like diversions evolved into profound learning experiences, equipping her with expertise that would later be invaluable for her work in radiation protection—a vital concern for astronaut safety. This ability to adapt and derive strength from detours is at the core of Dr. V's character.

When Vanessa joined NASA, she was excited to bring her interdisciplinary knowledge to the critical issue of genetic protection for astronauts. Yet, despite NASA's culture of innovation, she found her department hesitant to embrace new approaches, often limiting the scope of her contributions. Though initially discouraging, this experience clarified her vision for space health, sparking the realization that her work needed a broader, more adaptable platform. Determined to make a real impact, Dr. V established Space Exploration Strategies, a consultancy that collaborates globally to solve the complex health challenges of space travel.

Today, she leads her team with the same inner resolve

that guided the determined frog, transforming obstacles into momentum for progress. Dr. V's story is a testament to the power of resilience, showing that true innovation often requires trusting one's own path and vision, even when external voices urge otherwise. Through her work, she inspires others to pursue their own journeys, bringing humanity closer to a future where space exploration is safe and sustainable.

Dr. V's Journey to Self-Belief and Vision for Space Health

Dr. Vanessa Farsadaki's belief in a more inclusive future for space travel didn't come easily. It was shaped by her own journey through the often-exclusive world of space and medicine, where she frequently encountered obstacles that challenged her right to belong. Her own path, filled with unplanned detours and institutional barriers, showed her the importance of accommodating diverse backgrounds and skill sets in space health.

As Dr. V navigated the twists and turns of her career, her concept of "AstroMedicine" began to take shape. At its heart, AstroMedicine represents a democratized approach to space travel that is not limited to those with extreme physical conditioning but instead imagines a future where space is accessible to people from all walks of life. The development of this vision was a deeply personal process, grounded in her experiences of navigating systems not designed with diversity or inclusivity in mind. Through her resilience in the face of obstacles, she saw the need for a space health framework to support a broader spectrum of humanity.

Her passion for inclusiveness in space health blended with her growing understanding of how medical advancements made for space could benefit everyday life on Earth. Witnessing the transformative power of technology in healthcare, Dr. V came to see space health as a bridge between the distant stars and the immediate challenges faced by people on Earth. This idea empowered her, sparking a deep self-belief and commitment to making space health a driver for positive global change.

The Allegory of the Small Frog

The tale begins in a lush, vibrant forest, where the annual mountain race is the year's highlight, drawing a crowd of participants and spectators. Among the contenders is a small, unassuming frog whose quiet demeanor and diminutive size do little to inspire confidence among the onlookers. As the race commences, skepticism fills the air, with spectators vocally expressing their doubts. Shouts of "It's too steep for you!" and "You're too small to make it to the top!" echo through the trees, mixing with the natural sounds of the forest.

The race is grueling, with the path to the summit treacherous and fraught with obstacles. One by one, many frogs, dissuaded by the physical challenge and discouraged by the negative chorus from the crowd, begin to drop out. They gave in to the idea that reaching the summit is impossible, as the physical demands of the climb and the surrounding external doubt weaken their resolve.

However, the small frog continues its ascent, undeterred and seemingly oblivious to the growing skepticism and the dwindling number of competitors. With each determined leap, it moves steadily upward, its focus unwavering. As the frog advances, the crowd's shouts grow louder, urging it to accept defeat like the others. Yet, despite the noise and the challenging climb, the frog's pace remains steady. It appears to be in its own world, acting with an internal resolve that defies the spectators' skepticism.

As twilight approaches and the summit nears, a hushed silence gradually falls over the crowd. All eyes are fixed on the small frog as it approaches the final stretch. The air is tense with anticipation and slowly turns to awe as the frog makes its final leap to the peak, becoming the first and only contender to finish the race. The spectators' initial skepticism transformed into disbelief. Slowly, disbelief turned into admiration for the unexpected champion.

The other frogs, intrigued and inspired by the small frog's success, gather around to celebrate and inquire about how it maintained such focus and resilience in the face of overwhelming negativity. Then, it becomes clear that the small frog is deaf, having never heard any of the discouraging words. The frog thought that their gestures and shouting were cheering him on.

This story is a profound lesson on the power of self-belief and the importance of tuning out negative influences. The small frog's victory demonstrates that sometimes what appears to be a weakness can turn out to be one's greatest strength, especially when it allows focus and perseverance in pursuing one's goals. Dr. Farsadaki uses this narrative to remind us that we can often overcome our most significant challenges by simply believing in ourselves and steadfastly moving toward our goals, regardless of the doubts expressed by those around us. Just as her journey demonstrates how self-belief can evolve from adversity and a desire to broaden horizons for all, through her work, she shows aspiring scientists and doctors that innovation is not just about reaching further—it is about ensuring that everyone has a place in the journey forward, both in space and on Earth.

"We create our own destiny. Despite the cultural belief that our paths are predetermined, our actions, persistence, and willingness to step out of our comfort zones define our futures."

Desmond Fonyuy Wysenyuy

Desmond Fonyuy Wysenyuy's journey is a compelling example of how determination and self-belief can shape one's destiny, even when cultural norms suggest otherwise. Growing up in Kumbo, a small village in Cameroon, Desmond was surrounded by a society that valued stability and often believed that a person's fate was predetermined. This belief, deeply woven into the culture, suggested that individuals should accept the life they were given and resist aspirations that seemed "too ambitious" or "unrealistic." Desmond knew from a young age that he would have to break free from these expectations to pursue his dreams.

Determined to carve his own path, Desmond took a bold step in 2014, leaving Cameroon to study in Nigeria—an unusual and challenging move. Cameroon lacked a space agency or opportunities in space science, so he stepped outside his comfort zone to pursue his passion. This decision, unconventional in his community, was met with skepticism. Friends and relatives questioned why he would seek an education in a field with no apparent future in Cameroon. But Desmond's vision was clear: he believed that, with dedication, he could help shape the future of space exploration in Africa.

After earning a master's degree in space science and technology in Nigeria, he began his career as a scientific officer at the United Nations Economic Commission for Africa (UNECA). Over six years, he advanced to roles as a lecturer and project consultant, gaining recognition in his field. Yet, Desmond knew he needed to keep growing. This inner drive led him to pursue further education in the United States, where he believed new challenges and opportunities would accelerate his personal and professional development.

Throughout his journey, Desmond encountered self-doubt and skepticism from those around him, who often saw his aspirations as overly ambitious. Instead of yielding to discouragement, he cultivated mental resilience. Desmond's resilience was rooted in his ability to filter out negativity and focus on voices that empowered him. He surrounded himself with mentors and global peers who shared his vision for a brighter future in space exploration. Experienced leaders in space technology provided guidance and encouragement, reinforcing his belief that his goals were achievable and impactful.

In addition to mentorship, Desmond relied on techniques to reinforce his resolve. One powerful method was reframing challenges as building blocks rather than setbacks. Each barrier became an opportunity to prove his capability, and each small victory strengthened his belief that his path was one of his own makings. Desmond's approach to resilience also involved "mental filtering," where he consciously tuned out voices of doubt—cultural or personal—and amplified his mentors' and his peers' support and encouragement. This support system helped him focus on his potential and recognize that he could, in fact, create his own destiny.

Desmond's journey is a testament to the strength required to forge one's path, especially when cultural expectations suggest otherwise. He continues to inspire young Africans, showing them that while fate may shape the beginning of their stories, self-belief and resilience can redefine their futures. Through his unwavering dedication, Desmond challenges the notion of a predetermined path and proves that even the loftiest dreams are within reach when fueled by courage and a vision for change.

"Self-doubt is often the greatest barrier to realizing our true potential."

Vered Cohen Barzilay

Vered Cohen Barzilay's journey is a compelling tale of courage, innovation, and pursuing one's passion against the odds. Born into a Mizrahi Jewish family in Israel, Vered faced significant cultural and educational challenges from a young age. Despite these obstacles, she exhibited remarkable intellectual curiosity and initiative, teaching herself to read and write before most of her peers. This early display of autonomy marked her first step out of her comfort zone, challenging the educational norms expected of her.

As Vered grew, her educational pursuits highlighted her talents and desire to explore beyond the conventional paths laid out before her. Her passion for learning and her ability to self-educate uniquely positioned her at the crossroads of multiple interests, ranging from literature to technology. However, societal expectations and rigid educational structures often felt constraining, sowing seeds of doubt about her potential career paths.

Vered's career in journalism was groundbreaking, as she became Israel's first internet reporter, one of the country's first female police reporters, and a pioneering journalist at Israeli TV Channel 10. Throughout her career, Vered covered dangerous environments and high-profile legal trials, using her platform to address pressing societal issues and advocate for change. She co-founded a female journalist network that was recognized as 5th out of 100 most influential figures in the Israeli media.

Her strong passion for social justice led her to a career in a human rights organization, where she co-led global campaigns with famous artists such as Yoko Ono and U2. Vered also opened a publishing house specializing in human rights literature—a genre she invented—that was accepted by the most important universities in the world. She also published her first human rights novel. Later, Vered shifted her focus to promoting women's rights and was frequently invited to the Israeli parliament to speak on this critical issue.

Despite her success, Vered experienced an increasing disconnect with her endeavors as they did not fully align with her growing interest in science and technology—fields she was deeply passionate about but had initially set aside due to societal expectations and educational directions.

The turning point in Vered's career came when she pivoted back to her roots in science, technology, engineering, and mathematics (STEM), driven by the realization that her true passions lay in integrating STEM with the arts (STEAM). This decision was not made lightly; it involved stepping far out of her comfort zone, leaving behind a well-established career to venture into the uncertain terrain of educational reform.

Vered founded "Out of the Box," a global enterprise dedicated to redefining STEAM education by making it more inclusive, accessible, and aligned with the demands of the modern world. Her mission is to bridge the gap between traditional educational methods and the dynamic, interdisciplinary approaches needed in contemporary STEAM and aerospace fields.

"Out of the Box" identifies and nurtures talent across diverse environments globally, with a focus on "startup humans"—individuals whose potential to innovate transcends traditional boundaries. Its aim is to provide young people from all populations worldwide with top-level academic opportunities, practical tools, and knowledge, as well as connections to the aerospace communities. "Out of the Box" is committed to developing future aerospace leaders who excel in responsibility and possess high-level thinking and execution capabilities.

Vered's narrative is a testament to the impact of embracing one's passions and the transformative power of educational innovation. Her journey underscores the importance of challenging societal norms and the benefits of stepping out of one's comfort zone. Through her leadership, "Out of the Box" exemplifies how a single visionary, like Vered, can spearhead transformative initiatives that reshape entire fields. Just as figures like Elon Musk have revolutionized technology and space exploration, Vered nurtures the next generation of leading innovators, empowering them to pursue groundbreaking achievements.

Transforming Insights Into Action

Taking action on your goals requires **embracing your unique path**, developing resilience, and approaching challenges with determination. **Visualize your success,** and set clear, achievable goals that push your boundaries and lead to growth. Books like Valerie Young's *The Secret Thoughts of Successful Women* can offer valuable insights on overcoming imposter syndrome, helping you develop a strong sense of self-assurance as you pursue these goals.

In addition to setting goals, **harnessing the power of resilience** is critical. Even when setbacks occur, maintaining focus and perseverance is vital. Like the deaf frog in the race, one effective way to tune out negativity is by consciously redirecting your thoughts. When negative feedback or self-doubt arises, acknowledge it without letting it take root. Instead, focus on affirmations or past successes that reinforce your strengths.

Surrounding yourself with supportive mentors and peers can also act as a buffer, reminding you of your capabilities and goals.

The book *The Confidence Code* by Katty Kay and Claire Shipman explores how developing resilience, and confidence can help women overcome obstacles and push forward, even when faced with self-doubt.

One crucial step in overcoming self-doubt is identifying your self-limiting beliefs. Pinpoint the three most important ones holding you back, and reframe them with positive affirmations based on your achievements. For further guidance, Pauline Rose Clance's *The Impostor Phenomenon* provides tools for recognizing and dismantling imposter syndrome and practical advice for reframing negative thoughts. Seeking constructive feedback from trusted mentors is another way to build confidence and gain clarity on your strengths and areas for growth.

Surrounding yourself with a strong network of support helps unlock new opportunities and provides a foundation for growth. Engaging with resources like the Harvard Business Review article, *Stop Telling Women They Have Imposter Syndrome*, and TED Talks on confronting imposter syndrome will reinforce the importance of seeing your worth and asking for what you deserve. These resources offer both insight and inspiration on how to push past self-doubt.

Embrace scientific inquiry and critical thinking when faced with complex challenges. Applying an inquiring mindset can demystify difficult problems and help you devise practical solutions. Consider challenges as riddles that require investigation, testing, and evaluation. For example, *The Confidence Gap* explores how applying critical thinking to situations can help you push past perceived barriers and find innovative solutions.

Invest time in continuous learning by reading your field's latest research and publications. Stay engaged with professional organizations, such as Toastmasters International, to improve your communication skills and build leadership abilities. Mastering a critical skill that enhances confidence will make you more competitive in your industry. Leverage platforms like LinkedIn Learning's *Overcoming Imposter Syndrome* to stay sharp and prepared for new opportunities.

When overcoming self-doubt, take bold steps toward opportunities you may have previously hesitated to pursue. Whether applying for a new job, speaking up in meetings, or starting that exciting project, move forward with courage. Remember, as *The Confidence Gap* article explains, stepping into roles before you feel fully ready is often the key to success. Failure is not a setback but a vital part of growth and resilience-building.

As you continue to grow, share your experiences and insights with others. Resources like *The Impostor Syndrome Files* provide platforms for sharing stories, connecting with others, and finding support. Mentorship is a powerful tool for both giving and receiving guidance, offering mutual growth and encouragement.

Lastly, reflect on your progress and celebrate small victories. Every step forward brings you closer to achieving your goals. Embrace continuous growth and discovery, pushing beyond your comfort zone with confidence. Your unique talents and perspectives can transform your life—and the lives of those around you.

References

Clance, P. R. (1985). *The impostor phenomenon: Overcoming the fear that haunts your success*. Peachtree Publishers.

Corkindale, G. (2008, May 7). Overcoming impostor syndrome. *Harvard Business Review*. https://hbr.org/2008/05/overcoming-impostor-syndrome.

Desmond Tutu Quotes. (n.d.). BrainyQuote.com. Retrieved October 28, 2024, from https://www.brainyquote.com/quotes/desmond_tutu_454150.

Goerner, C. (2019, Oct. 4). *Overcoming Imposter Syndrome* [Video Course]. Linkedin Learning. https://www.linkedin.com/learning/overcoming-imposter-syndrome/the-reality-of-imposter-syndrome?u=99504138.

Imposter Syndrome Institute. (n.d.). *Impostor Syndrome Institute: Impostor syndrome experts*. Retrieved September 21, 2024, from https://impostorsyndrome.com/.

Kay, K., & Shipman, C. (2014, May 15). The confidence gap. *The Atlantic*. https://www.theatlantic.com/magazine/archive/2014/05/the-confidence-gap/359815/.

Kay, K., & Shipman, C. (2018). *The confidence code: The science and art of self-assurance—-What women should know*. HarperCollins.

Meninger, K. (Host) (2024). *The impostor syndrome files* [Audio Podcast]. https://www.kimmeninger.com/podcast.

Ramos, A. R. (2023, August 14). The deaf frog, Inspiring lessons. *Medium*. https://alexramos26.medium.com/the-deaf-frog-inspiring-lessons-ca0762e77fe1.

TED. (n.d.). *Fighting imposter syndrome* [Video Series]. https://www.ted.com/playlists/503/fighting_impostor_syndrome.

Tubman, H. (n.d.). *Quotable Quote*. Goodreads. Retrieved September 21, 2024, from https://www.goodreads.com/quotes/5935-every-great-dream-begins-with-a-dreamer-always-remember-you.

Tulshyan, R., & Burey, J.-A. (2021, February 11). Stop telling women they have imposter syndrome. *Harvard Business Review*. https://hbr.org/2021/02/stop-telling-women-they-have-imposter-syndrome?utm_medium=social&utm_campaign=hbr&utm_source=LinkedIn&tpcc=orgsocial_edit.

Young, V. (2011). *The secret thoughts of successful women: And men: Why capable people suffer from impostor syndrome and how to thrive in spite of it*. Crown Currency.

CHAPTER SEVEN CELESTIAL GARDENING: BLOOMING WHERE YOU ARE PLANTED IN THE GALAXY

"Bloom where you are planted. Embrace the present, engage fully with your responsibilities, and make a positive impact. Your current situation holds the potential for growth and fulfillment if you choose to see it."

Shelli Brunswick

B looming where you are planted is about recognizing and harnessing the potential in your current circumstances. It is not about waiting for the right moment or place but transforming the present into fertile ground for growth and success. Mahatma Gandhi wisely observed, "The future depends on what you do today."

This mindset teaches us that every situation, no matter how ordinary or challenging, holds the seeds of opportunity. Focusing on the present can create meaningful impact and personal fulfillment, leading to a sense of inspiration and motivation.

The philosophy of "bloom where you are planted" encourages us to see our current situation and any challenges not as a limitation but as fertile ground for growth. Theodore Roosevelt, the youngest person to become US President, summed this up perfectly when he said, "Do what you can, with what you have, where you are." Thriving is not about waiting for ideal circumstances but rather maximizing the opportunities right before us. Unexpected paths to growth and success can be discovered when you fully commit to your current reality.

True transformation begins when we channel our energy into the possibilities of today rather than dwelling on what might have been. As the ancient Greek philosopher Socrates once said, "The secret of change is to focus all of your energy not on fighting the old, but on building the new." This encapsulates the essence of thriving—embracing the present with intention and turning even the most ordinary roles into extraordinary platforms for growth.

True growth and success are not determined by our starting point but by how we nurture our environment. Visionary leaders understand this, demonstrating that greatness can be cultivated in the most unlikely places. By focusing on what can be done now, with the resources at hand, we set the stage for future success. This is where actual growth takes root— where the seeds of today's efforts bloom into the remarkable achievements of tomorrow.

Personal Reflections

Throughout my career, both in the military and civilian sectors, I frequently witnessed people yearning for past glories or dreaming of future roles, often overlooking the valuable opportunities right in front of them. Many colleagues believed that true satisfaction could only be found in more prestigious or glamorous assignments, like working on high-profile satellite or rocket projects. This mindset often led to disengagement and, ultimately, missed growth opportunities.

When I received my first assignment as a space acquisition officer, I was stationed in a space program office focused on ground stations, tasked with testing and verification—roles that were not considered the most thrilling in the space industry. Despite the initial lack of allure, I fully embraced this opportunity.

Working on ground stations offered me a unique chance to learn about digital twins and experience firsthand the critical importance of these facilities in satellite operations. My work took me across the United States, from overseeing upgrades at launch facilities at Kennedy Space Center and Cape Canaveral to Vandenberg Space Force Base and even to the remote landscapes of Greenland.

These experiences expanded my technical knowledge and deepened my understanding of the critical role ground stations play within the broader space ecosystem. By fully committing to the tasks, I experienced growth and fulfillment that exceeded my expectations. This dedication was recognized when I was selected as President of the Company Grade Officers Association (CGOA), an organization focused on supporting the professional development of junior officers.

Later, during that same assignment, I was honored to be named Company Grade Officer of the Year at Los Angeles Air Force Base (now Space Force Base). These significant career milestones reinforced for me that there will never be a better time than NOW to bloom where you are planted.

These experiences taught me that true satisfaction and success come from being fully present and engaged with where you are, not from chasing distant dreams. The grass isn't always greener on the other side; often, it's greenest where you choose to water it. By embracing each moment and maximizing the opportunities, I achieved personal advancement while significantly contributing to my community and industry. This journey taught me the importance of seeking guidance and learning from mentors. Their insights and support were invaluable in navigating the challenges of personal and professional growth, making me feel confident and supported.

Insights From Global Thought Leaders

"Stay focused on your purpose, trust in your abilities, and never underestimate the impact of your journey. You can overcome any challenge and inspire others to do the same."

Gabriella Goddard

Gabriella Goddard's journey demonstrates remarkable innovation, resilience, and adaptability. Growing up in Auckland, New Zealand, a country known for its outdoor lifestyle and can-do attitude, she was surrounded by the spirit of Kiwi ingenuity. This upbringing shaped her bold and adventurous outlook on life, instilling a deep sense of curiosity and drive.

Gabriella's career path didn't start with her eventual passion for coaching and space. Initially, she pursued a degree in food technology, with dreams of working in a chocolate factory. However, after a summer job in a candy factory, she realized that a lab-based career was not for her. Instead of being discouraged by this discovery, Gabriella pivoted and embraced new opportunities. This adaptability was a recurring theme in her life.

Gabriella's first overseas venture took her to Japan, where she immersed herself in a new culture, combining work in a New Zealand restaurant with Japanese language studies. This experience left an indelible mark, shaping her life's path in ways that would resonate for years to come. Afterward, she returned to New Zealand to launch her formal career in market research with AC Nielsen. Her role involved studying market trends and tailoring product strategies to the New Zealand market, an experience that sharpened her adaptability and analytical thinking. Her innovative thinking soon led her to Mexico, where she helped launch Nielsen's scanning service, marking her first significant international assignment.

In Mexico, Gabriella transitioned into product marketing, a role that refined her expertise in launching international products. After several successful years, she moved to the UK and played a crucial role in launching Europe's first broadband services. However, when the dot-com bubble burst, the company she worked for collapsed. This challenging moment became a turning point in her career. Instead of feeling defeated, Gabriella hired a coach to help navigate the uncertainty, a decision that led her to discover her true passion—executive coaching.

Gabriella has been an Executive Coach for over two decades, helping leaders and managers across industries foster creativity and innovation. Her philosophy is rooted in integrity, empathy, and the ability to view the world from multiple perspectives. Gabriella believes that trust, direct communication, and a visionary mindset are essential to leading in today's world.

A decade ago, Gabriella furthered her passion for creative thinking by launching the Brainsparker app, a "creativity coach in your pocket" (https://brainsparker.com). The app quickly gained global recognition and became a Top 10 creativity app in multiple countries, amassing over half a million users. More recently, Gabriella has focused her talents on the space industry, creating a leadership program through the UK Space Agency's LEO Entrepreneurial Accelerator, and later becoming a Mentor for this program.

Her story is a powerful reminder that growth comes not from following a single path but from embracing opportunities wherever they arise. Gabriella's journey exemplifies how challenges can lead to groundbreaking achievements when met with courage and creativity. By fully engaging in each chapter of her life and adapting to the circumstances around her, Gabriella shows that a willingness to grow in the present moment can be the ultimate pathway to success and fulfillment.

"Life is a series of choices that define our journey; each decision, whether small or monumental, shapes our path. Embrace opportunities, commit fully, and always align your choices with your values. This is how we leave a lasting impact and forge a meaningful legacy."

Karlton Johnson

Karlton Johnson's journey is a powerful example of blooming where you are planted. From humble beginnings to becoming the CEO of the National Space Society, his story showcases the importance of embracing opportunities and striving for excellence in any situation.

Born into a family of educators, Karlton developed a strong appreciation for learning and personal growth. His father, an educator and entrepreneur, instilled in him the value of education and the importance of being able to "walk with kings and queens but not lose the common touch." This lesson became a guiding principle throughout his life. Fascinated by space from a young age, Karlton spent hours reading the Encyclopedia Britannica, fueling his passion for space exploration.

Despite his initial reluctance, a chance encounter with an Army recruiter in college led Karlton to join the Air Force Reserve Officers' Training Corp (ROTC) ROTC program, marking the start of a distinguished military career. Early in his journey, a conversation with an Air Force personnel detailer transformed his outlook on assignments. He learned that success wasn't about choosing the perfect role but about being mission-ready and adaptable. This approach, coupled with commitment to duty, allowed him to bloom, excelling in roles ranging from pilot training to space and cyber operations. It shaped his approach to every assignment, no matter the challenges.

Karlton realized that any experience could be positive or negative, depending on the mindset. By seeing each role as an opportunity for growth, he thrived in even the most difficult conditions. His dedication to improving every situation earned him recognition and promotions, reinforcing the value of leaving every place better than he found it.

After retiring from the military, Karlton transitioned into the corporate world, applying the same philosophy of blooming where he was planted. He took on roles in advanced manufacturing and cyber risk management, leveraging his military experience to bring value to these new fields. His adaptability and dedication continued to demonstrate his resilience and versatility.

Mentorship has been another cornerstone of Karlton's journey. Throughout his career, he benefited from mentors who guided him in embracing each opportunity as a chance to grow, no matter the circumstances. In turn, he prioritized mentoring others, sharing his knowledge and experiences to help them succeed and learn to adapt and flourish wherever they are. This commitment reflects his belief in the power of community and support as essential elements in helping others bloom where they are planted, fostering resilience and adaptability in achieving their goals.

Karlton's leadership philosophy emphasizes integrity, service before self, and excellence—core values deeply instilled during his career in the United States Air Force. His story is a testament to resilience, adaptability, and a positive mindset—striving to make the most of every situation and leaving a lasting impact. These values not only guided him throughout his military service but continue to shape his approach to leadership in every role, ensuring that he remains grounded in ethical decision-making and committed to improving the lives of others.

> **"Your journey is uniquely yours, and every step, no matter how challenging, builds the foundation for your future. Embrace your passions, take risks, and never be afraid to chart your own path."**
>
> Mariam Naseem

Mariam Naseem's journey exemplifies resilience, adaptability, and the courage to pursue one's passions despite obstacles. Originally from Pakistan, Mariam moved to the United States to pursue an undergraduate degree in electrical engineering. Her fascination with space began early, sparked by her father's love for science fiction, notably Star Trek. This early exposure planted the seeds of a lifelong passion for space exploration. However, as an immigrant, she faced barriers in the US space industry due to the International Traffic in Arms Regulation (ITAR), which restricted her opportunities. With this limitation, Mariam temporarily set aside her space ambitions and chose to explore other fields.

Seeking adventure, she joined Schlumberger as a field engineer on an oil rig in Russia. This challenging experience taught her resilience, cultural integration, and how to thrive in extreme conditions. However, the cyclical nature of the oil and gas industry led to instability, and the 2016 downturn brought widespread layoffs. As Mariam faced uncertainty about her work visa, she decided to pivot. She applied for MBA programs in Canada, where a welcoming environment for international talent allowed her to chart a new course.

While pursuing her MBA at the University of Toronto, Mariam initially focused on technology project management, gaining experience in quantum computing and emerging technologies. However, her passion for space was reignited at conferences, where stories from female space entrepreneurs inspired her to reconsider her career path.

A pivotal moment came when a managing director at Accenture encouraged her to follow her passion for space. With support from mentors, Mariam tirelessly networked and applied for positions in the Canadian space industry, facing many rejections. Her perseverance paid off when she secured a role with a consulting firm working with the Canadian Space Agency (CSA). Despite taking a pay cut and moving to a new city, Mariam embraced this opportunity.

The COVID-19 pandemic brought new challenges, including job loss and uncertainty. But Mariam remained determined. She connected with nonprofit organizations like the Space Generation Advisory Council (SGAC) and the Open Lunar Foundation, gaining valuable industry insights. A scholarship to attend the Space Symposium allowed her to meet key figures, including the CSA's President, which led to a position on the CSA's industry relations team.

Mariam pursued an interest in space science, collaborating with a NASA Goddard Space Flight Center mentor on research related to icy ocean worlds and astrobiology. This collaboration and acceptance into six PhD programs culminated in her decision to join the University of Maryland to further her research and maintain her connection with her mentor at Goddard.

Throughout her journey, Mariam demonstrated the principle of blooming where you are planted by adapting to every challenge, leveraging her experiences, and pursuing growth opportunities. Her story highlights the power of resilience, risk-taking, and a strong support network in achieving one's dreams.

Transforming Insights Into Action

Personal and professional growth starts with **embracing the present** and **fully engaging** in your current responsibilities. By focusing on what you can control within your current situation, you begin to see the potential for development, turning challenges into opportunities. As Eckhart Tolle highlights in *The Power of Now,* being mindful of the present allows you to focus on opportunities rather than dwelling on what might have been.

Taking initiative and committing to your responsibilities sharpens your skills and enhances your visibility. This approach aligns with Greg McKeown's *Essentialism: The Disciplined Pursuit of Less*, which emphasizes focusing on what truly matters by discerning the vital few from the trivial many. Concentrating on the tasks at hand creates room for significant growth and advancement.

It is easy to fall into the **comparison trap**, constantly measuring yourself against others, but this often leads to dissatisfaction. Instead, focus on your unique journey and celebrate your progress. *Mindset: The New Psychology of Success* by Carol Dweck underscores the importance of maintaining a growth mindset, reminding us that growth happens when we focus on **our path** rather than comparing ourselves to others. This mindset allows you to recognize that each step you take, no matter how small, is an achievement worth celebrating.

Making a positive impact in your current environment is another key to flourishing. Even small, meaningful contributions—improving processes or supporting others—can lead to significant personal growth over time. As highlighted in Shawn Achor's *The Happiness Advantage*, cultivating positivity enhances your outlook and influences those around you, creating a more productive and fulfilling environment.

Proactively seeking ways to grow and contribute to your current sphere of influence is essential for unlocking your potential. Setting small, achievable goals helps maintain momentum and keeps you motivated. The article *How to Stay Focused When You Get Bored Working Toward Your Goals* by James Clear offers in-depth practical advice on staying committed even when the excitement fades, ensuring that you continue making progress.

To maximize your growth, seek feedback from trusted mentors and colleagues. This practice helps you stay on course and reveals areas for improvement. Additionally, it is important to maintain curiosity and creativity, which fuel long-term personal and professional success.

One effective way to protect your sense of curiosity is to set aside moments for "awe breaks"—intentional pauses to appreciate something inspiring or beautiful, such as a scenic view or a favorite piece of music. These breaks can shift your mindset, refresh your creativity, and help filter out negativity. The article, *Why You Need to Protect Your Sense of Wonder— Especially Now*, from Harvard Business Review has excellent suggestions for encouraging curiosity, creativity and awe.

Now is the time to root yourself in the present and start blooming. Take ownership of your growth, make a positive impact, and watch as you transform your life and those around you. The journey to a fulfilling and enriching life begins now— right where you are.

References

Achor, S. (2010). *The happiness advantage: The seven principles of positive psychology that fuel success and performance at work*. Crown.

Achor, S. (2011, May). *The happy secret to better work* [Video]. TED Conferences. https://www.ted.com/talks/ shawn_achor_the_happy_secret_to_better_work? subtitle=en&trigger=0s.

Clear, J. (n.d.). How to stay focused when you get bored working toward your goals. *James Clear*. https://jamesclear.com/ stay-focused.

Dweck, C. (2015, July 16). The growth mindset: Talks at Google [Video]. YouTube. https://www.youtube.com/watch? v=-71zdXCMU6A.

Dweck, C. S. (2007). *Mindset: The new psychology of success*. Random House Publishing Group.

Gandhi, M. (n.d.). *Quotable Quote*. Goodreads. Retrieved September 21, 2024, from https://www.goodreads.com/ quotes/806111-the-future-depends-on-what-we-do-in- the-present.

Laipply, J. (2010, April 1). RSA Animate: Drive: The surprising truth about what motivates us [Video]. YouTube. https:// www.youtube.com/watch?v=u6XAPnuFjJc.

McKeown, G. (2014). *Essentialism: The disciplined pursuit of less*. Crown.

Ritchie, D. (2022, October 24). The best 101 inspirational quotes about change you'll ever read. *Calendar*. https:// www.calendar.com/blog/the-best-101-inspirational- quotes-about-change-youll-ever-read/.

Roosevelt, T. (n.d.). *30 Best Theodore Roosevelt quotes with image*.

Bookey. Retrieved September 21, 2024, from https://www.bookey.app/quote-author/theodore-roosevelt.

White House Historical Association. (n.d.) *Theodore Roosevelt: The 26th president of the United States*. The White House. https://www.whitehouse.gov/about-the-white-house/presidents/theodore-roosevelt/.

Tolle, E. (2004). The power of now: A guide to spiritual enlightenment. Namaste Publishing.

Fessell, D.P. and Karen Reivich. (2021, August 25). Why you need to protect your sense of wonder—Especially now. *Harvard Business Review*. https://hbr.org/2021/08/why-you-need-to-protect-your-sense-of-wonder-especially-now.

CHAPTER EIGHT COMMAND CENTRAL: WHY THE FRONT ROW HOLDS THE KEYS TO YOUR LAUNCH

"Sitting in the front row isn't just about being seen; it's about being ready to seize every opportunity, engage actively, and lead boldly."

Shelli Brunswick

I n both our professional and personal lives, positioning is everything. Just as a spacecraft's trajectory is determined by its launch position, our success is deeply influenced by where we choose to place ourselves—both literally and figuratively. The front row symbolizes more than just a seat; it represents leadership, presence, and a proactive attitude. It is a deliberate choice, a statement of intent, and a strategic advantage that can propel us toward our greatest potential.

Queen Elizabeth II wisely remarked, "I have to be seen to be believed," capturing the essence of visibility and presence in achieving success. Sitting in the front row is not just about being seen—it is about leading, seizing opportunities, and maximizing potential by being close to the action. It is about positioning yourself where you can open doors to new possibilities and more significant influence.

Sitting in the front row is akin to standing at the starting line of a race with the best possible view and focus. This decision is more than just selecting a seat—it is a mindset that cultivates proactivity, engagement, and visibility. When you place yourself in a prime position, you enhance your learning, making it easier to absorb and understand the material. However, the benefits extend beyond learning; they include increased visibility to leaders, mentors, and potential collaborators. Your commitment becomes evident, opening doors to new relationships and opportunities.

This deliberate positioning also signals your enthusiasm and dedication, influencing how others perceive and engage with you. Amelia Earhart shrewdly noted, "The most difficult thing is the decision to act; the rest is merely tenacity." Taking that step to the front builds confidence, helps you overcome social anxieties, and nurtures personal growth and resilience.

Sitting in the front row places you at the forefront of interactions, ensuring you are in a critical position to ask questions, interact with speakers, and engage in discussions. This proactive stance is particularly significant in space exploration and leadership, where innovation and bold thinking are essential.

By positioning yourself at the leading edge—whether in meetings, research projects, or industry events—you increase your chances of making meaningful contributions and being recognized for your efforts. This empowerment is a key aspect of the front-row mindset, giving you control over your career and personal growth.

The power of the front row isn't just a concept—it is a principle that has profoundly shaped my journey. In this chapter, I will share personal reflections on how embracing this mindset transformed my career, from my early days as a young airman in the US Air Force to leading in the space industry. You will also hear from global thought leaders who have harnessed this same approach to propel their careers, demonstrating how this strategy transcends industries and geographies, offering a universal blueprint for success. The path to success is shaped by where you choose to stand today—position yourself for liftoff and watch your career soar to new heights.

Personal Reflections

Even as a nine-year-old in Ms. Waldusky's fourth-grade class,

I was naturally drawn to the front row. Each day, I arrived at school with a sense of excitement, eager to absorb every lesson and engage fully with my peers and teachers. But my enthusiasm was not limited to academic learning; it was about immersing myself in every environment, embracing every opportunity to connect, learn, and grow.

This habit of active participation became a guiding principle in my life, manifesting consistently, whether in classrooms, leadership training sessions, or at major conferences. This sense of connection and engagement is a key part of the front-row mindset, making you feel more involved and connected.

This commitment to sitting in the front row was pivotal throughout my early career as a young airman. I always chose the front row during leadership training programs, knowing it would allow me to absorb crucial information more effectively and engage directly with instructors. This proactive approach did not just enhance my learning; it also caught the attention of senior leaders and mentors, setting the stage for my future in the Air Force.

As I advanced in my career and became an officer, the principle of front-row engagement continued to serve me well, particularly during space program reviews. Sitting in the front row was not just about being seen—it was about fully engaging with the content, asking the right questions, and demonstrating my dedication to the mission. One particularly memorable instance occurred during a critical Air Force Satellite Control Network briefing. My active participation in the front row led to a mentorship opportunity with senior officers, significantly shaping my career trajectory in the space industry.

When I transitioned to the private sector and took on leadership roles, including my positions as Chief Operating Officer, Founder, Chief Executive Officer, and a member of several Boards of Directors, I carried this front-row mentality with me. Whether in team meetings, boardrooms, or industry presentations, I made it a point to sit in the front row, signaling my commitment and support. This visible leadership boosted my team's confidence and set an example others could follow. Being in the front row demonstrated the importance of active participation and engagement, inspiring my colleagues to do the same.

An excellent example of how this approach has made a difference is my experience at the International Astronautical Conference. Day after day, I occupied a front-row seat, attentively following each speaker. My engagement was evident —I nodded, smiled, took diligent notes, and shared insights on social media. By the conference's end, my proactive involvement had not gone unnoticed; an organizer commended me with an 'A' in attention. This moment embodies my lifelong practice of staying at the heart of the action, where visibility and engagement create opportunities and where leadership by example encourages others to step up and engage.

My journey highlights the significant impact visibility and active participation can have on a career. Sitting in the front row is more than just choosing a seat—it embodies a leadership mindset, engagement, and a commitment to seize every opportunity. Doing so will advance your growth and set a powerful example for others.

Insights From Global Thought Leaders

"I call myself a front-row woman. If there's no chair for you at the table, bring your own. Always raise your hand, share your ideas, and make every moment count. We must stop sitting in the back and take charge of our narrative."

Linda Pereira, PhD

Linda Pereira's journey is a remarkable narrative of determination, resilience, and leadership. Born in Britain to a humble family, Linda's parents worked for a noble household connected to the royal family. Her mother was a housekeeper, and her father handled various tasks around the estate. Growing up, Linda witnessed the grand events and gatherings from a distance, which fueled her ambition to rise above her circumstances.

From a young age, Linda was determined to be part of the world she observed through the crack in the door. Her mother instilled in her the importance of education, hard work, and perseverance. This guidance solidly grounded Linda and enabled her to excel academically, earning a full scholarship to King's College, London, one of the top universities in the UK.

After completing her studies, she started her career as a salesgirl at Marks and Spencer, a well-known British retail chain. Her exceptional sales skills and dedication quickly garnered attention, and the company's board offered her further education and a career in management in exchange for a five-year commitment. However, Linda had bigger dreams. She turned down the offer, choosing instead to pursue opportunities aligned with her vision for a more impactful career.

In line with her vision, Linda secured an internship at the royal household as an event coordinator for Queen Elizabeth II. Linda had always taken a "front-row" approach, actively seeking out experiences that would expand her perspective. Determined to learn from the best, she networked strategically and applied a detailed proposal on how she could contribute to the royal household's operations. Her commitment to excellence and willingness to take risks paid off, and she was accepted.

Working at the palace was more than an internship—it was a masterclass in discipline, discretion, and poise. Surrounded by leaders and dignitaries, Linda's front-row attitude allowed her to absorb invaluable insights into protocol and diplomacy, setting her apart in ways that would prove critical in her next role. This experience directly catalyzed her transition to the European Parliament, where her expertise in handling high-stakes events and her familiarity with diplomatic decorum were assets in strategic communication.

For the next five years, Linda worked across Strasbourg and Brussels, applying the lessons she learned at the palace to navigate international relations and complex diplomatic situations. Each challenge was an opportunity to reaffirm her front-row attitude, actively engaging, asking questions, and viewing every project as a chance to grow her expertise and build her network.

Linda's career flourished as she moved into the corporate world, focusing on brand placement and activation. She approached each opportunity as a chance to make an immediate impact. Her strategic communication expertise and her ability to navigate diverse cultural environments with finesse quickly set her apart. Linda confidently took on high-profile clients and managed large-scale events, seeking out roles that challenged her and pushed her to grow.

Throughout her journey, Linda encountered significant obstacles. Determined to stay engaged and lead from the front, she launched her own company while raising two young daughters, often balancing family responsibilities with long hours to build her business. Events like 9/11, the economic crisis of 2008, and the unexpected loss of her business partner in 2017 tested her resilience. In each instance, Linda faced these challenges head-on, adapting and finding innovative ways to thrive instead of stepping back.

During the COVID-19 pandemic, Linda's event-focused business faced yet another critical challenge. Refusing to be sidelined, she embraced the shift to virtual engagement, upskilling her team in digital communication and launching online training programs to keep her business relevant. Her proactive response sustained her business and allowed it to grow in a transformed marketplace. Linda's willingness to adapt and lead by example demonstrates the power of perseverance and forward-thinking.

Linda's guiding "Rule of 12" captures the essence of a front-row mentality, emphasizing the importance of making powerful first impressions. She believes that the first 12 seconds when you enter a room, the first 12 steps you take, and the first 12 words you speak shape how others perceive you. This principle aligns with her belief in always being fully present and purposeful, ensuring that every interaction demonstrates confidence and authority, whether in meetings, events, or casual encounters. Through her actions and principles, Linda has positioned herself as a leader in her industry, showing others how to bring their best selves to every opportunity and exemplify a front-row presence wherever they go.

Linda's story is a testament to how a front-row mindset can shape a career, showing that she continuously positioned herself for impactful and transformative roles on the global stage by choosing to sit in the front.

> "Sitting in the front row means being at the forefront of change. It's about being visible, proactive, and ready to seize every opportunity. My career has allowed me to build influential networks and stay ahead of industry trends."
>
> Piotr Trabinski

Piotr Trabinski's journey exemplifies a life of ambition, resilience, and adaptability. Born in Poland during a time of political and economic upheaval, he was deeply influenced by his father's active role in the anti-communist movement. This environment of resistance and hope instilled in Piotr an understanding of the importance of standing up for one's beliefs and taking decisive action. Observing his father's courage and commitment, Piotr learned early on that challenging the status quo and positioning oneself at the forefront of change are crucial to making a real impact. These early experiences fueled Piotr's determination to pursue a life marked by forward-thinking and opportunity, ultimately shaping his own journey as he moved from Poland to the United States, aiming high and sitting metaphorically—and often literally—in the front row throughout his career.

Back in Poland, Piotr's drive for excellence propelled him through his academic career, where he consistently positioned himself at the forefront of his studies, ultimately pursuing a law degree. During his studies, he developed an interest in financial law, which opened the door to his first professional role in the banking sector. Piotr's proactive approach and curiosity about emerging financial technologies led him to a position in

Allied Irish Bank's Direct Banking department, where he focused on developing technology-driven products. His enthusiasm for innovation helped him secure this role, demonstrating his willingness to engage deeply with the evolving landscape of finance.

Following the global financial crisis, Allied Irish Bank rebranded as Santander, and Piotr continued to explore the intersection of finance and technology, recognizing an opportunity to address the growing concerns around digital security. His interest in protecting clients from internet crime was sparked during an internship in the United States, where he delved into the nascent field of cybersecurity. Driven by a front-row mentality, he actively pursued projects that allowed him to deepen his expertise, leading to published research and a co-authored book on internet security from a policy perspective.

Determined to expand his knowledge and fulfill his dream of returning to the United States, Piotr enrolled in the Institute of World Politics and later George Washington University, where he studied computer science and cybersecurity. His passion for staying ahead in his field led him to the International Monetary Fund (IMF), where he applied his interdisciplinary skills in law, finance, and cybersecurity. Piotr's commitment to impactful leadership at the IMF allowed him to rise through the ranks, ultimately becoming an Executive Director representing nine countries, including Switzerland, Poland, and several Central Asian nations. In this role, he advised on macroeconomic policies, digital currency, and emerging technologies, always seeking to position himself at the forefront of innovative policy development.

After the IMF, Piotr launched his consultancy company specializing in digital money, blockchain technology, and national security payment systems. His expertise quickly garnered attention from major organizations, leading him to advise the World Bank on digital transformation and development finance. His work expanded to tackle global issues, including advising on Ukraine's reconstruction alongside

European investment funds and development banks.

Piotr's commitment to being at the cutting edge of industry trends has been central to his success, allowing him to maintain a competitive edge and navigate rapid technological changes. He credits much of his success to the strategic choice to sit in the "front row," ensuring he remains seen, heard, and engaged with key industry players.

> "Many of my opportunities came by sitting in the front row and not taking a backseat. It's about being present and engaged. When I was writing my first book, sitting in the front row at a conference led to a chance meeting with Jeff Gitomer, who ended up writing the foreword for my book."
>
> Sandy Carter

Sandy Carter's career journey is a compelling narrative of resilience, adaptability, and proactive engagement that defines authentic leadership. Her path, marked by unexpected turns and strategic pivots, offers valuable lessons on the importance of being present and ready to seize opportunities.

Initially inspired by her father's passion for space, Sandy dreamed of becoming an astronaut. She attended space camps and immersed herself in the realm of space exploration, fueled by a sense of wonder and curiosity. However, a series of personal experiences shifted her focus. The loss of her grandmother and a close friend to cancer led her to pursue a career in medicine. She enrolled at Duke University to become a doctor.

Life, however, had other plans. Sandy discovered she had an allergy to chemicals used in medical environments, which caused her to pass out. This unexpected hurdle was devastating, but it also became a turning point. Seeking guidance, Sandy consulted her advisor, who held dual roles at the medical center and the newly formed computer science department. He suggested she explore computer science as an alternative path.

Embracing this new direction, Sandy wrote her senior thesis on using computer simulations to test drugs, a project that combined her interests in problem-solving and technology. This pivot set the stage for her successful career in the tech industry. Over the years, Sandy's professional path has spanned startups and major corporations, including International Business Machines Corporation (IBM) and Amazon Web Services (AWS), where she contributed significantly to innovation and leadership.

One of the defining moments in Sandy's career occurred during a conference when she worked for IBM. Noticing that the front rows were empty, she sat in the front row—a simple yet powerful decision that exemplified her proactive approach. During the event, she actively tweeted about the speaker's comments. To her surprise, after the presentation, the speaker, Jeff Gitomer, a renowned author, approached her to express his gratitude for her engagement. He appreciated her real-time feedback, which he had monitored during his talk.

This chance encounter led to a significant career opportunity. Sandy mentioned she was writing a book, and Jeff offered to read it, write a quote and the foreword, and promote it to his extensive email list. This support helped her book achieve bestseller status almost instantly, demonstrating the power of strategic positioning and active engagement.

Sandy was pivotal in starting a program for space startups at AWS. She worked with innovative companies, tackling challenges such as finding water on Mars and corralling space debris. Her involvement in these projects advanced technological solutions and highlighted the potential of space exploration to address global issues. One notable project involved partnering with a team to define requirements for a rover mission to Mars, showcasing her ability to bridge technical and strategic aspects of space missions.

Sandy has held various executive positions, including Chief Operating Officer, Chief Marketing Officer, Chief Sales Officer, Channel Chief, and Chief Product Officer. Her versatility and willingness to embrace different roles reflect her adaptive leadership style and commitment to continuous learning.

Sandy's story is about how strategically positioning yourself and actively engaging can help you attain professional achievement and personal growth. Sandy has seized opportunities and significantly impacted both the tech and space industries. Her experiences have taught her the value of resilience, the importance of being proactive, and the power of literally and metaphorically sitting in the front row.

Transforming Insights Into Action

Achieving real growth in your career is about taking what you've learned and turning it into actionable steps. The front-row mindset goes beyond where you physically sit—it is about how you position yourself in every aspect of life and work. It is about being proactive, visible, and ready to seize opportunities as they arise.

To begin, consider where you are in your career or personal journey. Visualize the key events, meetings, or opportunities on your horizon where your presence could significantly impact your future. **Strategic learning** starts with positioning yourself for success. You maximize your focus and information retention by sitting in the front row, whether at a conference or in a team meeting. This step allows you to fully engage with the material, ensuring that you're absorbing everything that can help you grow.

But it is not just about learning; **enhanced visibility** is another benefit of placing yourself at the front. Leaders, mentors, and potential collaborators are more likely to notice you when you are in the spotlight. This leads to more opportunities to connect, network, and make lasting impressions. By being visible and engaged, you are signaling your commitment to your field and demonstrating that you are ready to take on bigger challenges. Queen Elizabeth's motto, "I have to be seen to be believed," reflects the power of visibility in leadership.

Of course, **active engagement** is critical in this approach. By actively participating—asking questions, contributing insights, and interacting with others—you learn more effectively and show others that you are invested in your growth. This makes you stand out as someone ready to take charge and contribute meaningfully. Jim Collins' *Good to Great* delves further into how great leaders make strategic decisions that lead to long-term success.

For many, sitting in the front row can initially feel uncomfortable, but this discomfort is where growth happens. **Building confidence** comes from overcoming initial anxieties and proving to yourself that you belong in those front seats. The more you embrace these situations, the more your confidence grows and the more natural it becomes to step into leadership roles.

Moreover, being at the forefront puts you in the perfect position to **seize opportunities**. When you are in the front row, you are closer to the action and able to capitalize on opportunities faster than if you were on the sidelines. Whether it is a chance to meet an influential person or to contribute to a significant discussion, you will be ready to take advantage of these moments. For those interested in innovation and leadership, Sandy Carter's *Extreme Innovation 3: Superpowers for Purpose and Profit* is a valuable resource for learning how to seize opportunities and lead effectively.

Finally, this proactive positioning helps you cultivate essential **Leadership Development**. By consistently choosing the front row, you are developing **a growth mindset** and leadership qualities that will set you apart. You are positioning yourself to be seen as a leader, both by your peers and by those in higher positions of authority. If you are looking to lead in a rapidly evolving tech landscape, *The Tiger and the Rabbit: Harnessing the Power of the Metaverse, WEB3, and A.I. for Business Success* by Sandy Carter offer strategies to stay at the forefront of cutting-edge technologies.

As you increase your visibility, use it as a springboard to expand your professional network. Contact colleagues, mentors, and leaders who can help you grow. Building and strengthening these connections can open doors to new opportunities and collaborations, making networking a powerful tool in your career advancement.

To stay inspired and continue learning from leaders who embrace the front-row mindset, explore the IgnitedThinkers' *Space Champion Interview Webinars*. These interviews with leaders in the space industry offer powerful, in-depth lessons on positioning yourself for success.

Finally, keep up with leadership and innovation insights from experts like **Sandy Carter** by following her contributions on Forbes. If technology and innovation are more your focus, *Tech Blueprint* by Piotr Trabinski offers valuable guidance for staying at the forefront of industry trends.

The journey to success begins with a choice to position yourself at the forefront, where visibility and opportunity converge. Sitting in the front row is not just about physical placement—it is about taking command of your career and being intentional in your actions. It is about actively stepping into the spotlight, engaging, and embracing every chance to learn, grow, and lead.

As you move forward, remember that every decision to be visible, take action, and seize opportunities shapes your trajectory. Taking a prominent position represents a launchpad for your ambitions, where you can maximize your potential and set the course for your future. The opportunities are vast, and your potential is limitless.

Now is the time to take your seat at the forefront. Be bold in your choices, be proactive in your engagements, and be confident in your ability to lead. The expanse of your career is waiting for you to explore it—so position yourself for liftoff and reach for the stars.

References

Amelia Earhart Quotes. (n.d.) BrainyQuote.com. Retrieved October 28, 2024, from https://www.brainyquote.com/quotes/amelia_earhart_120929.

Carter, S. (n.d.) Contributors. *Forbes.* https://www.forbes.com/sites/sandycarter/.

Carter, S. (2009). *New language of marketing 2.0: How to use ANGELS to energize your market.* IBM Press.

Carter, S. (2017). *Extreme innovation 3: Superpowers for purpose and profit.* Param Media.

Carter, S. (2023). *The Tiger and the Rabbit: Harnessing the Power of the Metaverse, WEB3, and A.I. for Business Success.* Wiley.

Collins, J. (2001). *Good to great.* Harper Business.

Gitomer, J. (2004). *The Little Red Book of Selling.* Bard Press.

IgnitedThinkers. (n.d.) *Space champion interview webinars* [YouTube channel]. www.youtube.com/@IgnitedThinkers.

Trabinski, P. (2024, Jan 12) Introducing "Tech Blueprint," An inclusive space for tech enthusiasts, the intrigued and the concerned. *Tech Blueprint.* https://piotrtrabinski.substack.com/p/introducing-tech-blueprint.

Windsor, E. A. M. II. (n.d.) *30 Best Queen Elizabeth quotes with image.* Bookey. Retrieved September 21, 2024, from https://www.bookey.app/quote-author/queen-elizabeth-ii.

CHAPTER NINE ALIGNING THE STARS: EMBRACING MINDFULNESS IN THE ASTRAL DANCE

"Mindfulness is about being present and fully engaged with the infinite possibilities around us. My journey has taught me that by embracing each moment with awareness and clarity, we can navigate challenges, transforming obstacles into opportunities and dreams into reality."

Shelli Brunswick

In our relentless, fast-paced world, finding moments to pause, reflect, and connect deeply with ourselves and the universe can feel like a luxury. The constant barrage of work deadlines, social media notifications, and an ever-growing to-do list pulls us in countless directions, leaving us overwhelmed, stressed, and disconnected from what truly matters. Yet, amidst this chaos lies a powerful antidote: mindfulness. It is the practice of being fully present and engaged in the current moment, without judgment or distraction.

Mindfulness is a transformative force. It is a lifeline that allows us to reclaim control, restore balance, and rediscover the joy of being present. The growing body of scientific research supporting mindfulness is a testament to its profound advantages, from lowering stress and anxiety to enhancing focus. By paying attention to the present moment with full awareness, curiosity, and compassion, we unlock a reservoir of benefits that reach far beyond mere tranquility.

Jon Kabat-Zinn, creator of the Mindfulness-Based Stress Reduction (MBSR) program, perfectly encapsulates mindfulness: "Mindfulness means paying attention in a particular way: on purpose, in the present moment, and nonjudgmentally." This approach encourages us to fully engage with the present, shedding the weight of past regrets and future anxieties. It cultivates the empathy and insight needed to navigate life's challenges, transforming obstacles into opportunities and dreams into reality.

Oprah Winfrey, a renowned media executive and philanthropist, offers simple yet profound advice: "Breathe. Let go. And remind yourself that this very moment is the only one you know you have for sure." Her words emphasize the importance of presence and acceptance, reminding us that the power of now is all we truly possess. This mindset is central to developing self-awareness, allowing us to be fully present in our relationships, and attuned to the emotions of those around us.

Mindfulness is not about disengagement; it is about engaging more fully with life's challenges and opportunities. It sharpens our ability to prioritize, helping us distinguish between what is truly important and what is merely urgent. It is a powerful tool for managing our emotions and empathizing with others. As Daniel Goleman, a renowned expert on emotional intelligence, explains, "Feeling emotions is what makes life rich. You need your passions." Mindfulness allows us to engage with our emotions deeply, and understand them without being overwhelmed. This state is crucial for developing social intelligence and ultimately leads to stronger, more meaningful relationships.

Incorporating mindfulness into our daily lives is not just about reducing stress; it is about finding stillness amidst the chaos. As Deepak Chopra advises, "In the midst of movement and chaos, keep stillness inside of you." This stillness is our anchor, empowering us to navigate life's complexities with clarity, resilience, and purpose, leading to greater personal and professional success. Moreover, mindfulness enhances our creativity, focus, and overall well-being, setting the stage for a more fulfilling life.

By integrating mindfulness into our lives, we reclaim our sense of balance and transform our approach to life and work, turning challenges into opportunities and living with a deeper understanding of purpose and fulfillment.

Personal Reflections

In the whirlwind of our fast-paced world, finding that elusive still point where I could focus on what truly mattered to me—such as writing this book—became a challenge that demanded my conscious embrace of mindfulness. This practice was not just a technique; it became my sanctuary, a refuge that allowed me to silence the clamor of endless emails, social media pings, and the seductive lure of multitasking.

I often reflect on a quote by Paulo Coelho: "When you say 'yes' to others, make sure you're not saying 'no' to yourself." This wisdom became my guiding light as I embarked on writing this book. For years, colleagues and friends encouraged me to share the lessons and insights I had gathered from my work in the space and technology sectors. Yet, it was easy to get swept away in the constant motion of 'doing'—mentoring emerging professionals, diving into new projects, and always saying 'yes' to the next opportunity.

Then came the realization: I needed to prioritize my endeavors and focus on my goal and the impact I wanted to make. This book was not just another project; it was a long-held dream, a piece of my voice waiting to resonate in the world's libraries. To bring this dream to life, I had to live the very principles I was writing about—mindfulness and emotional intelligence. I began politely declining requests that threatened to divert my focus, even for causes close to my heart. I trimmed my commitments, ensuring every 'yes' I said aligned with my core goals.

Mindfulness became the cornerstone of my writing process. Each session was a deliberate ritual, a space where I could immerse myself fully in the flow of ideas without the intrusion of distractions. This discipline was not just about managing external noise but about an internal recalibration of my priorities. It was about recognizing that to contribute meaningfully to the world, I first had to honor my aspirations and navigate relationships with empathy and insight.

Through this focused practice, I discovered that mindfulness was more than a stress reduction technique—it was a profound connection with my work and an essential tool for enhancing my resilience and adaptability. Each decision, each word written, became a deliberate choice, infused with clarity and purpose. The result was a completed manuscript and a transformed approach to life and work that balanced productivity with peace and heightened emotional awareness.

As we navigate the frenetic symphony of modern life, mindfulness acts as both a shield and a compass. It protects us from the distractions that threaten our focus and guides us through the complexities of personal and professional demands. In a professional setting, mindfulness can help us manage stress, enhance our decision-making abilities, and improve our relationships with colleagues and clients. It empowers us to distinguish between what is urgent versus what is important, allowing us to dedicate ourselves fully to the pursuits that truly matter and nourish our souls.

Insights From Global Thought Leaders

"Mindfulness is not merely a practice but a profound connection to the timeless wisdom of our ancestors. It's about understanding that every moment holds the potential for greatness, and every breath we take can be a step towards realizing our deepest strengths."

Machiko Gozen

In the quiet mountains of Kagoshima, Japan, the Gozen family has cultivated green tea for over 400 years. Machiko Gozen, the 13th generation of samurai women, grew up amidst the serene tea fields, absorbing the wisdom of her ancestors. Her grandmother, a formidable woman embodying the samurai spirit, instilled in Machiko the principles of bushido—discipline, honor, and a deep sense of responsibility to serve humanity.

From a young age, Machiko understood that the essence of mindfulness was not merely in meditation but in every action she took. Her grandmother's teachings were clear: "A mindful heart is a warrior's greatest weapon." This philosophy guided Machiko as she navigated the complexities of modern life while preserving her cultural heritage.

Machiko's journey took her across continents, eventually leading her to the vibrant city of Dubai, where she showcased the integration of mindfulness in business practices at the Dubai Expo. Her presence was calming, her words deliberate, and each sentence was a testament to her deep understanding of mindfulness.

Taking over the Vendôme Tea Group, Machiko transformed it into a beacon of mindfulness and empowerment. Under her leadership, the company grew into one of the largest quality tea exporters in the world, with plantations in Japan, Sri Lanka, and France.

Her approach to mindfulness was rooted in the samurai tradition. "In battle, clarity of mind and calmness were essential for survival. These principles help us navigate the corporate world with grace and wisdom." For Machiko, mindfulness was a strategic tool that enhanced cognitive and emotional resources, enabling leaders to make thoughtful decisions and lead with empathy.

Machiko created the foundation Femmes du Monde and the project Tea for Two. These initiatives were born from her belief in the power of a simple cup of tea to inspire kindness and altruism. "For each box of tea sold, we offer a free cup to someone in need. This act of giving is a moment of mindfulness, a pause to reflect and connect," she explained.

Machiko's philosophy extended beyond individual practice to encompass community mindfulness. She believed in the power of collective mindfulness, where groups engage in mindful practices together, enhancing their collective intelligence and cooperation. This communal approach was evident in her efforts to empower women in the tea plantation communities, providing them with opportunities for education and entrepreneurship.

Machiko's story of overcoming challenges through mindfulness is particularly inspiring. She shared the difficulties she encountered while introducing sustainable practices to tea farming, facing uncertainties such as financial risk, cultural resistance, environmental factors, and market acceptance. Despite fear and doubt, Machiko fostered a mindful approach, allowing her to navigate these complexities with clarity and composure. By staying grounded and present, she reduced anxiety, managed stress, and made thoughtful decisions, ultimately enhancing her ability to perform under pressure and achieve long-term success.

A central theme in Machiko's teachings was the power of kindness. She emphasized that true strength lies in being kind, even in the face of adversity. "Being kind is the greatest form of strength," she often said. This philosophy helped her maintain calm and composure, even when dealing with difficult people or situations. Instead of reacting angrily, Machiko responded with kindness, seeing it as a way to transform negative energy into positive outcomes.

Machiko's narrative was not just about the past but a vision for the future. She saw mindfulness as a bridge connecting her cultural heritage with modern leadership practices. "Mindfulness connects us with the strength and integrity of past generations, carrying forward their wisdom to create a better tomorrow," she said.

As Machiko shared her journey, her words resonated deeply: "Mindfulness is about being fully present and aware, not just in meditation but in every action, every decision. It is about understanding that each moment holds the potential for greatness."

Machiko's story is a testament to the transformative power of mindfulness, a bridge between the ancient wisdom of the samurai and the dynamic challenges of the modern world. Her journey from the tea fields of Kagoshima to the global stage encapsulates the essence of embracing mindfulness in the astral dance of life and leadership.

"Mindfulness transforms how we move through life, allowing us to fully engage with each moment and each movement. It is the bridge between the mind and the body, creating harmony and balance in all we do. Being focused, disciplined, and consistent every single day is crucial. Building good habits is more important than finding a cure, and cultivating emotional intelligence is essential as we work with people."

Adam Dipert

Adam Dipert's journey is one of remarkable intersections—between science and art, physics and dance, and mindfulness and movement. Born in a small town in Ohio, Adam's early life was marked by a rebellious streak and an insatiable curiosity. However, his career eventually led him to deeply understand the mind-body connection and the necessity for mindfulness in all his activities.

Despite feeling disengaged and struggling in high school, Adam found solace and excitement in the world of circus arts. After graduating, he did what any adventurous soul would do—he joined the circus. For several years, Adam traveled across North America, mastering skills in juggling, stilt walking, acrobatics, and fire dancing. These years were about performance and understanding the intricate connections between physical movement and the natural world.

Adam eventually went to Ohio State University, where he discovered that the principles he practiced in the circus were deeply intertwined with the mathematical concepts taught in his physics classes. "In math class, we talk about things moving through space or rotating, and it seems complex unless you realize it's related to the world we experience," Adam explains. This realization was a turning point, allowing him to see the seamless integration of art and science.

Adam continued his education at Arizona State University, where he pursued advanced degrees in physics. Adam also explored zero-gravity movement, conducting experiments that married his passion for physics with his background in circus arts.

His studies and performances together taught him that mindfulness bridges the mind and body, creating harmony and balance in all we do. "Mindfulness transforms the way we move through life, allowing us to fully engage with each moment and each movement," Adam shares. He believes mindfulness allows for a deeper connection with the present moment, enhancing physical performance and intellectual engagement.

"The process of learning to be open about where we are in our lives, both personally and in our society, is crucial," Adam notes. This openness, he believes, is essential for innovation and creativity, whether in the circus ring or the laboratory. His performances and teachings emphasize that mindfulness bridges the mind and body, creating harmony and balance in all we do.

"Mindfulness is about being focused, disciplined, and determined. It's about being consistent every single day," Adam emphasizes. For Adam, being present means not diverting extra bandwidth to distractions and fully committing to the task at hand. "Building good habits is more important than finding a cure," Adam asserts. He believes cultivating emotional intelligence (EQ) is essential, and his approach to mindfulness and movement strengthens his ability to connect with others on a deeper level.

By embracing mindfulness, Adam has navigated his unique path with grace and clarity, transforming obstacles into opportunities and dreams into reality. His ability to overcome academic challenges and integrate seemingly disparate fields into a cohesive career is a testament to his innovative spirit.

Adam's journey from Ohio to the forefront of space research and performance art is a powerful narrative of how mindfulness can transform lives. His story highlights the importance of being present, embracing challenges, and integrating diverse passions into a fulfilling career.

"Opportunities are not just about seizing what comes your way but actively shaping the path you want to walk on. Know yourself, know

your values, and let them guide you towards opportunities that promise success and fulfill your deepest convictions."

Tuana Yazıcı

Tuana Yazici's journey shows how discipline, creativity, and resilience can shape an extraordinary life. Born in Istanbul, Turkey, she grew up in a family where education, creativity, and perseverance were central values. Her mother, an architect, artist, and author, and her father, an economist, instilled in her a deep appreciation for intellectual and artistic pursuits. From an early age, Tuana demonstrated an exceptional blend of creativity and discipline, hosting her first art exhibition at just four years old and publishing her first book by the age of seven.

Tuana's life took a significant turn when her family moved to the United States when she was nine. The transition was challenging, as she had to adapt to a new culture and learn new languages, including English and French, on top of the German she had already mastered at an Austrian school in Turkey. However, instead of becoming overwhelmed, Tuana embraced the experience mindfully, staying present and accepting each challenge with patience and openness. By approaching these obstacles with curiosity and resilience, she maintained a calm focus that allowed her to thrive in her new environment. Her mindful attitude helped her stay grounded and find stability amidst the change, demonstrating how mindfulness can transform even the most daunting challenges into opportunities for growth.

Tuana's academic achievements reflect her drive to excel. She graduated from the University of Miami a year early with a degree in Philosophy, Politics, and Economics (PPE) and a minor in Psychology. Never one to settle, she completed a two-year master's program in International Administration, specializing in International Space Law, in just one year. Now, she is preparing to take the Florida Bar while managing her businesses and nonprofit organizations.

Her professional accomplishments are as impressive as her

academic ones. Tuana founded several organizations, including the Tuana Group, AeroAI Voyages, AeroAI DesignLab, and AeroAI Guardian. AeroAI Guardian is a standout project that uses reconnaissance satellites to monitor international human and wildlife trafficking hotspots, highlighting her commitment to using technology for humanitarian and environmental causes. Her ventures reflect her innovative spirit and ability to combine mindfulness with action, focusing on purposeful work that benefits others while staying true to her values and guiding principles.

Discipline has been a constant in Tuana's life. She started piano lessons at age three and a half, a passion she continues today, and pursued ballet for 11 years while engaging in martial arts training. These physical activities provided her with a balance between mind and body, reinforcing the importance of mindfulness in action.

Her deep love for animals has been a driving force behind much of her work. This passion inspired her to write and illustrate four children's books on protecting animals and the environment. One of her books became a bestseller in Turkey, and she donated all the profits to animal charities.

Tuana's pursuit of knowledge did not stop with formal education. She spent her summers studying at prestigious institutions such as Harvard, Oxford, and Cambridge, broadening her global perspective and building a network of international connections. Despite her many accomplishments, she remains grounded. She always approaches life with a clear and present mindset, focused on the task at hand while keeping her values at the forefront of everything she does.

Tuana's journey demonstrates the power of mindfulness, resilience, and discipline. She has turned challenges into opportunities, maintaining clarity of purpose throughout her life. Her story reminds us that success is not just measured by achievements but by staying true to one's values and using each moment as an opportunity for growth. Through her work, Tuana inspires others to embrace mindfulness, lead with purpose, and turn obstacles into springboards toward a meaningful future.

Transforming Insights Into Action

Mindfulness is not just a practice—it is a powerful tool that can enhance every aspect of your personal and professional life. **Integrating mindfulness into your daily routine** can sharpen decision-making, increase empathy, and build resilience. Start small by dedicating 5–10 minutes daily to mindful breathing or meditation. As you grow more comfortable, gradually extend these sessions until mindfulness becomes a cornerstone of your daily routine. Whether eating, walking, or simply pausing to breathe, use these moments to center yourself and become fully present.

Mindfulness is also an opportunity to **leverage your cultural heritage and traditions**. By connecting with and honoring the values of past generations, you can foster a more mindful approach to life and work. These traditions can provide grounding and clarity, helping you create a meaningful connection between your past and your future. This conscious awareness, deeply rooted in culture, can be a powerful tool for shaping your daily decisions.

A vital aspect of mindfulness is **practicing self-awareness and gratitude**. By reflecting regularly on your strengths, areas for growth, and the support systems around you, you will gain clarity in your career and personal life. Self-awareness keeps you authentic and grounded, while gratitude ensures you focus on the positives, allowing you to navigate challenges with resilience.

Mindfulness is not limited to stillness. It can be integrated into **physical activities such as yoga and tai chi**, enhancing mental and physical well-being. These practices bridge the gap between art and science, fostering creativity and innovation. Being mindful during physical movement can boost performance and unlock new ideas. *Mindfulness in Plain English* by Bhante Henepola Gunaratana is a valuable guide on integrating mindfulness into various aspects of life.

Rather than seeking quick fixes, **focus on building good habits** that prioritize consistency and long-term growth. Mindfulness helps you develop emotional intelligence and resilience and manage stress effectively. Daily mindfulness practices create sustainable habits that enhance your overall well-being. Greater Good Science Center offers extensive resources on building habits rooted in mindfulness and emotional intelligence.

As you continue your journey, consider embracing the transformative power of mindfulness and emotional intelligence in every aspect of your life. Engage with your surroundings and the people in your life by being fully present. **Prioritize what truly matters** by clarifying your values and focusing on one task at a time. Set healthy boundaries that protect your well-being and take mindful breaks to recharge. Cultivating a habit of gratitude can bring more joy and fulfillment, not only in your work but also in your personal life. Andy Puddicombe's TED Talk, *All it Takes is 10 Mindful Minutes*, is a wonderful starting point.

Every moment presents an opportunity to be fully present, to connect deeply with yourself and those around you, and to make intentional choices that align with your values. Embracing these practices will help you become more resilient, focused, and connected. Shauna Shapiro's TED Talk, *The Power of Mindfulness: What You Practice Grows Stronger*, provides further insights into the impact of mindfulness on resilience and focus.

Living with intentional awareness is more than a practice; it is a profound shift in how we engage with the world. It encourages us to be fully present and to approach each moment with clarity and purpose. This mindset allows us to see beyond immediate challenges, transforming them into opportunities for growth and self-discovery. By embracing this approach, we cultivate a deeper connection with our true selves, aligning our actions with our core values and aspirations.

The beauty of being fully present lies in its simplicity and power. It teaches us to pause amidst life's busyness, breathe, and find stillness within. This stillness is not about disengagement but fully engaging with what matters most. By cultivating this awareness, we open ourselves to a more prosperous, more meaningful life—one where we navigate the complexities of modern living with grace and resilience.

As you continue your journey, let mindfulness be the foundation upon which you build a life of purpose and fulfillment. In these moments of intentional presence, we find the strength to pursue our passions, the clarity to make deliberate choices, and the compassion to connect deeply with others. With this approach as your guide, you can transform your everyday experiences into a path toward a brighter, more meaningful future.

References

Arab News, Japan. (2022, March 8). *Eight influential Japanese women to celebrate this Women's Day.* Arab News, Japan. https://www.arabnews.jp/en/features/article_67302/.

Farah, D. (2021, May 16). *From France to Japan: How a samurai woman took over French tea house Janat Paris.* Arab News, Japan. https://www.arabnews.jp/en/features/article_44347/.

Farah, D. (2022, February 21). *A piece of the Eiffel Tower is now at Expo 2020 Dubai.* Arab News, Japan. https://www.arabnews.jp/en/features/article_66174/.

Goleman, D. (2005). *Emotional intelligence: Why it can matter more than IQ.* Random House Publishing Group.

Goleman, D. (2013, November 2). *Daniel Goleman on focus: The secret to high performance and fulfilment* [Video]. YouTube. https://www.youtube.com/watch?v=HTfYv3IEOqM.

Gunaratana, H., & Gunaratana, B. (2011). *Mindfulness in plain English: 20th anniversary edition.* Wisdom Publications.

Naik, P., Harris, V., & Forthun, L. (2019, Nov. 25). *Mindfulness: An Introduction.* University of Florida, IFAS Extension. https://edis.ifas.ufl.edu/publication/FY1381.

Palouse Mindfulness. (n.d.). Mindfullness-Based Stress Reduction. Online MBSR/Mindfulness (Free). Retrieved September 24, 2024, from https://palousemindfulness.com/.

Puddicombe, A. (2012, November). *All it takes is 10 mindful minutes* [Video]. TED Conferences. https://www.ted.com/talks/andy_puddicombe_all_it_takes_is_10_mindful_minutes?subtitle=en&trigger=0s.

Shapiro, S. (2017, March 10). The Power of Mindfulness: What You Practice Grows Stronger | Shauna Shapiro | TEDxWashingtonSquare. YouTube. Retrieved September 24, 2024, from https://www.youtube.com/watch?v=IeblJdB2-Vo.

TED. (2022, March 22). *Teach circus, learn math | Adam Dipert* [Video] YouTube. https://www.youtube.com/watch?v=zSx_iKRBo_s.

The Space Juggler. (n.d.). *Home.* Space Juggler.com [Video channel]. https://www.thespacejuggler.com/videos.

University of California, Berkeley. (n.d.). Greater Good Science Center. Retrieved September 24, 2024, from https://ggsc.berkeley.edu/.

Yazici, T. (2021). Analysis: Legal Barriers Complicate Future in Orbit. *The Space Report, 4,* 47-52. https://www.thespacereport.org/wp-content/uploads/2022/01/TSR-Q421-Book_PROD4.pdf.

Yazici, T. (2022, June). A proposal for the usage of reconnaissance satellites to monitor international human and wildlife trafficking hotspots. *Acta Astronautica, 195,* 77-85. DOI: https://doi.org/10.1016/j.actaastro.2022.02.012.

CHAPTER TEN STELLAR VIRTUES: HARNESSING PASSION, PERSEVERANCE, AND PATIENCE FOR GALACTIC SUCCESS

"Passion ignites our dreams, perseverance turns them into reality, and patience sustains us through the journey. Together, these virtues empower us to overcome obstacles, embrace growth, and achieve greatness."

Shelli Brunswick

Embark on a journey through the vast cosmos of professional challenges, where three stellar virtues—passion, perseverance, and patience—serve as your guiding stars. These qualities are not just traits; they are essential forces that ignite ambition, strengthen resolve, and sustain your voyage toward success. Whether navigating the space industry or charting a course in other fields, these virtues are not just for a select few but for everyone, regardless of your career path or life journey. They are the keys to transforming dreams into reality and breaking through barriers to reach new frontiers of growth and fulfillment.

In pursuing personal and professional success, passion is not just the fuel; it is the engine that drives our enthusiasm and commitment, propelling us to overcome challenges and pursue our aspirations. It sparks creativity, inspires others, and propels us forward, even when the path seems daunting.

Sam Walton, founder of Walmart, once said, "If you love your work, you'll be out there every day trying to do it the best you possibly can, and pretty soon everybody around will catch the passion from you—like a fever." This contagious energy is not just the foundation of great achievements: it is the catalyst that sets the stage for perseverance and patience to work their magic.

Perseverance is the unwavering determination to keep moving forward despite setbacks. Long-term success often requires sustained effort over years, sometimes decades, to bring a vision to life. Whether it is an engineer refining a design, an entrepreneur navigating the ups and downs of launching a startup, or a policy advocate pushing for systemic change, perseverance builds resilience, strengthens character, and turns failures into learning opportunities.

The legendary basketball player Kobe Bryant emphasized this when he said, "Great things come from hard work and perseverance. No excuses." In the expansive universe of career aspirations, it is common to begin with enthusiasm, only to encounter doubts and setbacks. In these moments of uncertainty, the true power of perseverance reveals itself.

Patience, the third pillar of this triad, is the art of waiting with a positive attitude, trusting the process, and appreciating the journey. In the space industry, patience is essential for navigating the complexities and long timelines inherent in exploration. However, the need for patience goes beyond space; it is crucial in any sector where significant achievements require time, collaboration, and careful planning. The renowned primatologist and conservationist Jane Goodall captured this sentiment perfectly: "Without patience, I could never have succeeded." As humanity sets its sights on returning to the Moon, exploring Mars, and venturing beyond, patience becomes even more critical.

These monumental endeavors in space serve as a powerful example, but the principles of patience, perseverance, and passion are just as vital in any career or profession.

Through personal stories and insights from global thought leaders, this chapter offers the inspiration and strategies to harness the forces of passion, perseverance, and patience, enabling you to overcome obstacles and achieve your goals. By integrating these interstellar virtues, we can navigate the ever-changing landscape of our careers, unlock our potential, and leave a lasting impact on the world. Whether expanding humanity's presence in the cosmos or striving for success in any area, let passion, perseverance, and patience be your launchpad as you chase and capture the stars, one determined step at a time.

Personal Reflections

When I first gazed up at the night sky as a young girl, I felt an undeniable connection to the cosmos—a connection that would chart the course of my life. The stars seemed to beckon me, whispering of endless possibilities and a universe brimming with potential. This initial spark of wonder ignited a passion that guided me through every challenge and triumph in my career. My journey, beginning with the disciplined demands of the US Air Force and evolving into roles that have continuously pushed the boundaries of space advocacy, education, and leadership, has been defined by three guiding virtues: passion, perseverance, and patience.

Passion has been the driving force behind every move, fueling my ambitions and propelling me forward, even when the path was steep and uncertain. This burning desire to explore and innovate has been the light that guided me through some of the most challenging phases of my career. Whether I was crafting policies and legislation on Capitol Hill alongside members of Congress, managing cutting-edge technology programs as a program manager, or inspiring acquisition professionals as a professor at Defense Acquisition University, my passion for space and its boundless opportunities has been the constant flame lighting my way. But passion alone was not enough; perseverance turned this passion into meaningful, tangible achievements.

Perseverance has been my steadfast companion, the engine

that powered me through obstacles, helping me to keep moving forward despite setbacks and failures. As a space acquisition officer, I learned valuable lessons in perseverance while working on complex projects like satellites, ground stations, and launch systems. Navigating long-term projects taught me to focus on the end goal by breaking down tasks and maintaining motivation. In the space industry, where multi-year projects and complex challenges are the norm, perseverance is not just a virtue but a necessity. It enabled me to see projects through to completion, even when the finish line seemed distant and elusive. This unwavering determination allowed me to navigate the many hurdles inherent in space initiatives and ensured that I maintained focus and resilience over the years.

Patience, often the most undervalued of the three virtues, has been a critical component of my success. In a field where significant advancements can take years, if not decades, to materialize, patience has taught me to trust the process, value incremental progress, and remain steadfast in pursuing far-reaching goals. Whether I was creating pathways for underrepresented groups in science, technology, engineering, art, and mathematics (STEAM) careers or developing new programs to help more entrepreneurs and investors find their way into the space industry, I knew that patience was key. These efforts were not just about immediate results but about unlocking economic opportunity and fostering workforce development on a global scale.

My work has also been about inspiring generations to pursue careers in space, STEAM, and innovation by sharing my own story and journey—helping to create both the current and future workforce. My incredible collaborations with trailblazers at various international organizations have further enhanced this journey. Together, we have worked tirelessly to expand access, create opportunities, and empower the next generation of leaders. This harmonious blend of passion, perseverance, and patience has shaped my journey and guided me through countless challenges and triumphs.

Throughout my career, I have drawn inspiration from a quote by Theodore Roosevelt, the 26th President of the United States, known for his robust leadership and vision. While in the Air Force, my stepfather gave me a plaque with this powerful quote, and its meaning has stayed with me.

"It is not the critic who counts; not the man who points out how the strong man stumbles, or where the doer of deeds could have done them better. The credit belongs to the man who is actually in the arena, whose face is marred by dust and sweat and blood; who strives valiantly; who errs, who comes short again and again, because there is no effort without error and shortcoming; but who does actually strive to do the deeds; who knows great enthusiasms, the great devotions; who spends himself in a worthy cause; who at the best knows, in the end, the triumph of high achievement, and who at the worst, if he fails, at least fails while daring greatly, so that his place shall never be with those cold and timid souls who neither know victory nor defeat."

This quote has been a constant source of resolve, reminding me to pursue my best, follow my passions with all my heart, and recognize that achieving greatness requires perseverance and patience to endure. My journey has always been about more than just personal success; it has been about leaving the world better than I found it. In addition, it has been about ensuring that opportunities within the space industry are accessible to everyone.

Insights From Global Thought Leaders

"Empower a woman, and she can change the world."

Lumbie Mlambo

Lumbie Mlambo's journey is a profound testament to the power of passion, perseverance, and patience. The youngest of eleven children, she experienced a childhood steeped in love and community in rural Zimbabwe. Her mother, a beloved schoolteacher, was her greatest inspiration. As a compassionate and dedicated educator, her mother taught academic lessons and instilled values of resilience and service that went beyond the classroom through support for her students and the community. Lumbie often saw her mother spend extra hours helping those in need, a devotion that engrained in Lumbie a lifelong commitment to uplifting others.

A pivotal influence on Lumbie's life was her father, a man of remarkable strength and kindness. An orphan who never had the opportunity to attend school, he nonetheless built a life dedicated to humanitarian work. His deep-rooted compassion and unwavering commitment to serve those around him left an indelible mark on Lumbie. Through his example, she learned that education and status are not prerequisites for making a meaningful difference in the world. His legacy of service fueled her mission to continue his work, focusing on providing clean water and sanitation to underserved communities—a mission born out of her parents' shared values of resilience, dedication, and selfless service.

Lumbie's path was not without its challenges. She faced numerous obstacles, from bureaucratic hurdles to health crises. One significant health challenge was a stroke she suffered at a young age while in Zimbabwe. With limited medical resources available, doctors gave her a slim chance of survival if she stayed. The decision to travel to the United States for treatment was fraught with risk, but Lumbie's resilience and the support of her family saw her through to recovery. This near-death experience fueled her determination to make a meaningful impact, recognizing that her survival had given her a second chance to fulfill her purpose.

Her passion for improving lives through clean water access led her to establish the JB Dondolo nonprofit organization in honor of her father. The organization focuses on removing barriers to clean water, sanitation, and hygiene in impoverished communities. One of JB Dondolo's notable achievements is installing a water filtration system, which serves over 20,000 people in the Igusi community in Zimbabwe. This project provides essential clean water, restores dignity, improves school attendance for girls, and helps reduce infant mortality rates.

Lumbie's perseverance is evident in her relentless pursuit of funding and supporting the project. Despite facing skepticism and stereotypes about the misuse of funds in Africa, she persisted. She creatively leveraged small donations, grants, and innovative fundraising methods, such as online auctions of student artwork and book sales, to finance her initiatives. Her perseverance paid off when she received support from significant organizations like the Tony Elumelu Foundation, which provided mentorship and funding, helping her expand her impact.

Patience was a critical virtue in Lumbie's journey. Establishing and growing a nonprofit organization, especially one focused on complex issues like clean water and sanitation, requires long-term commitment and the ability to navigate setbacks. Lumbie has demonstrated remarkable patience in securing funding, building partnerships, and implementing sustainable solutions. Her work with the *100 Voices for Our Planet* initiative, a United Nations Water Action Agenda Progress Report, brings together global leaders and advocates to promote environmental sustainability and climate action, emphasizing sustainable living and environmental consciousness. This initiative highlights her understanding that lasting change takes time and collective effort.

Lumbie's story is a powerful example of how passion, perseverance, and patience can drive transformative change. Her commitment to improving lives through access to clean water, as well as her ability to overcome personal and professional challenges, inspire others to pursue their goals with the same fervor and resilience. As she continues to empower women and communities, her legacy grows, reflecting the profound impact of one individual's commitment to making the world a better place.

"Passion is the rocket fuel that powers my journey through the cosmos of both aviation and life. It transforms everyday challenges into opportunities for growth and innovation, guiding my trajectory beyond

the stars. I strive to pass this same energy to the next generation, inspiring them to reach for their own skies with zeal and determination."

Klaus von Storch

Klaus Von Storch's journey into the cosmos began in Chile, a country with no formal space program. Born on February 20, 1962—the day John Glenn orbited the Earth—Klaus was surrounded by the energy of the space race from his earliest years. His father, passionate about aviation, took him frequently to an air club where Klaus learned about aircraft up close. Meanwhile, his aunt in the United States sent him patches from NASA's space missions and a treasured photograph of the Apollo 11 crew, sparking an insatiable curiosity for space exploration. These mementos of the Apollo missions filled his young mind with wonder, shaping a dream that would drive his future.

At just 16, Klaus joined the Chilean Air Force, pursuing his fascination with aerospace and eventually becoming a fighter pilot. The Air Force selected him to become the first Chilean astronaut candidate. To advance Chile's satellite and space ambitions, Klaus was sent to the University of Southern California to study aerospace engineering, a significant step that brought him closer to the world of space. But even as his path began to take shape, Klaus would face a life-altering challenge in the skies—one that would test his courage and resilience to the core.

A tragic midair collision that claimed the lives of Klaus' co-pilot, as well as the pilots of the other plane, left Klaus deeply shaken, a painful reminder of aviation's risks and the fragility of life. As the sole survivor, Klaus emerged knowing two things. First, to live each day with purpose, recognizing that life's unexpected challenges demand both courage and acceptance, a belief strengthened further when he later lost his brother in an aviation accident. Second, he learned that the mind has an "emergency mode" that gave him heightened clarity, allowing him to execute life-saving actions instinctively. Returning to flying was emotionally challenging, but with each flight, Klaus's commitment grew stronger, turning his journey into a tribute to those he lost and a testament to perseverance.

Years after the midair collision, Klaus had the rare opportunity to welcome Neil Armstrong to Chile for FIDAE, an international air and space conference. In their meeting, Klaus felt an immediate connection with Armstrong, whose tales of the Apollo missions—marked by near-catastrophic challenges, setbacks, and historic achievements—resonated deeply. Inspired, Klaus shared his story of survival from the collision and ejection, describing how it tested his courage and forged a stronger sense of purpose. Armstrong listened with empathy, understanding the fine line between survival and loss. This encounter reignited Klaus's passion for space and reinvigorated his commitment to pushing boundaries. Armstrong's unwavering dedication to progress reminded Klaus that even the loftiest goals are achievable with resilience, courage, and vision—qualities that would continue to guide him as he pursued new frontiers in aviation and aerospace.

Although Klaus never traveled to space himself, he came close, being considered for both a Space Shuttle flight and a Soyouz mission. While these plans did not come to fruition, Klaus made significant contributions to space exploration, including the groundbreaking "Ladybugs in Space" experiment aboard NASA's STS-93 Mission. This experiment studied the effects of microgravity on biological relationships, an essential concept for future space exploration and human habitation. The project allowed students to observe ladybugs and aphids in space and compare their behavior to similar experiments on Earth. The experiment demonstrated that ladybugs could adapt and function in space, advancing scientific understanding and inspiring young minds. Klaus's commitment to education and public engagement was evident through this initiative.

Patience was another critical virtue Klaus exemplified throughout his career. He learned that achieving significant milestones in space exploration often required years of preparation, collaboration, and the ability to endure setbacks.

His role in operating Chile's first satellite and coordinating the Ladybug Experiment involved meticulous planning and focusing on long-term objectives.

Navigating the complex regulatory and funding landscapes of space projects also required patience. Klaus's ability to collaborate with stakeholders and regulatory agencies contributed to the success of his endeavors. He understood the importance of building solid relationships and valuing others' contributions to achieve productive outcomes.

Without a formal space agency in Chile, Klaus had to rely on passion and perseverance to advance his space career. Despite the obstacles he faced, his leadership through logistical and governmental hurdles demonstrated his unwavering commitment to his goals, highlighting the essential role of resilience in achieving long-term success.

Klaus's journey is a testament to how passion, perseverance, and patience work together to create a path to success in the challenging field of space exploration. His passion sparked his journey, perseverance kept him moving through obstacles, and patience allowed him to navigate space missions' long and complex processes. Klaus's legacy is not just in his achievements but in the inspiration he provides for future generations, encouraging them to pursue their dreams with resilience and determination.

"My journey has taught me that true strength lies in embracing our passions, persisting against all odds, and patiently working towards change, even when the path is difficult. As the first female mechanical engineer in my community, I know that every barrier broken is a step forward, not just for myself, but for all the women who will follow. It's about more than achieving our own dreams—it's about lifting others as we rise."

Asta-Adji Sadou

Asta-Adji Sadou's journey is a profound example of how passion, perseverance, and patience can shape a life dedicated to breaking barriers and making a lasting impact. Born into the Fulani indigenous community in Cameroon, Asta grew up in a world marked by significant challenges. The Fulani, a semi-nomadic pastoralist community, have long struggled with issues such as land disputes, climate change, and violence from extremist groups like Boko Haram. These challenges have often led to the displacement and marginalization of her people, particularly women, who face additional barriers to education and participation in public life.

Her supportive parents strongly encouraged Asta to pursue her passion for education despite these formidable obstacles. As the only daughter in her family, she knew from an early age that her academic success could be a powerful example for others in her community, especially women and girls. However, her journey was fraught with difficulties. Her father's family opposed her education, fearing that it would expose her to risks and threaten traditional gender roles. The opposition was so intense that family members even threatened her mother.

In the face of such adversity, Asta's father made the courageous decision to send her abroad for her education. This move was a turning point in Asta's life, enabling her to escape the immediate dangers at home and pursue her dream of becoming an engineer. Asta's passion for mechanical engineering propelled her to excel in her studies, leading her to become the first female mechanical engineer in her community —a remarkable achievement in a society that often confines women to domestic roles.

Returning to Cameroon, however, brought a new set of challenges. The societal norms and stereotypes she had briefly escaped while studying abroad now confronted her again. Asta struggled to find a job that matched her qualifications because mechanical engineering was not considered a profession for women. But instead of being disheartened, Asta's perseverance kicked in. She knew that her path was not just about personal success but about paving the way for other women in her community.

With this resolve, Asta founded a cooperative society focused on education, gender equality, sustainable development, and innovative approaches to mitigate the effects of climate change. Her organization works with the Fulani community to address pressing issues such as access to education, land use, and women's empowerment. Through her work, Asta has become a beacon of hope and a role model for young women. She showed them that breaking free from traditional constraints and pursuing their dreams is possible.

Asta's ability to integrate her skills and interests in ways that serve her aspirations and her community's needs is a testament to her innovative spirit. Her passion for mechanical engineering and sustainable development drives her to create solutions that benefit her people and contribute to the broader goal of environmental sustainability. However, her patience allows her to navigate the slow and often challenging process of societal change. She understands that true transformation takes time, and her efforts to advocate for gender equality and educational opportunities for women will pay off in the long run.

Asta's story powerfully reminds us that passion, perseverance, and patience are virtues and essential tools for those who seek to make a difference in the world. Her journey is one of resilience and determination. She showcases how these qualities can empower individuals to overcome even the most daunting obstacles and create lasting change.

Transforming Insights Into Action

As you embark on your personal and professional journey, **passion**, **perseverance**, and **patience** will serve as your foundation. These three virtues work together to guide you through challenges, allowing you to unlock your potential and reach new levels of success.

Passion is the driving force behind your aspirations. Following what genuinely excites and motivates you will help you overcome obstacles and keep you moving forward, even when the path becomes difficult. In *Grit: The Power of Passion and Perseverance*, Angela Duckworth emphasizes how passion fuels your commitment to long-term goals, making it easier to stay focused when the journey becomes tough.

However, passion alone isn't enough; **perseverance** must complement it. This is the unwavering determination to push through setbacks and obstacles. Developing perseverance means being willing to keep going even when progress feels slow, or challenges seem insurmountable. It involves setting small, achievable goals, building resilience in adversity, and refusing to give up on your dreams. James Clear's *Atomic Habits* provides valuable strategies for turning perseverance into lasting habits by breaking larger goals into smaller, actionable steps to ensure you stay on track.

Along with passion and perseverance, **patience** is essential for maintaining composure and focus over the long haul. Success rarely happens overnight. It requires the wisdom to trust the process, even when results are not immediately visible. Patience helps you appreciate the journey, recognize incremental progress, and remain steadfast as you work toward far-reaching goals. M.J. Ryan's *The Power of Patience: How This Old-Fashioned Virtue Can Improve Your Life* delves into this often-undervalued virtue, showing how patience allows you to keep sight of your aspirations while waiting for the right opportunities to unfold.

Incorporating these virtues into your daily life can create **transformative results**. First, identifying what excites you will help you integrate passion into your daily routine. When you align your activities with your passions, your work will feel more fulfilling, and you will naturally be more driven to overcome obstacles. As Daniel H. Pink explains in *Drive: The Surprising Truth About What Motivates Us*, real motivation comes from within. It goes beyond traditional rewards and stems from doing work that aligns with your internal values and passions. Setting small, consistent goals allows you to persevere through difficult moments by focusing on achievable steps rather than getting overwhelmed by the bigger picture. The key lies in discipline and consistency—each small, deliberate action strengthens your commitment and steadily propels you toward greater achievements.

While working toward your goals, cultivating patience will help you manage the inevitable delays and setbacks that come with any meaningful endeavor. Tracking your progress and celebrating small wins can reinforce your patience. **Journaling** can be a helpful tool, allowing you to reflect on how these virtues—**passion**, **perseverance**, and **patience**—are shaping your journey and what adjustments might be necessary.

Although not a primary focus of this chapter, at the same time, you must remember the importance of **self-care**. Physical and mental well-being are vital to sustaining your energy and resilience, enabling you to continue pushing forward. Adequate sleep, regular exercise, and mindfulness practices help to balance your ambitions with the need for restoration. These routines ensure you do not burn out while working toward your dreams. Self-care habits will reinforce the idea that success is about thriving during the process as well as reaching the finish line.

The triad of passion, perseverance, and patience forms the bedrock of lasting success. Passion ignites our dreams and fuels the journey, providing the energy to move forward, even when the road is challenging. Perseverance gives us the strength to rise after each setback, transforming failures into valuable lessons and pushing us toward our goals. Patience, though often underestimated, grants us the wisdom to understand that true achievement takes time, allowing us to remain composed and focused as we progress.

Success is not a destination but a continuous process of growth and learning. Each step forward offers a chance to build new skills, gain insights, and strengthen your resolve. By embracing passion, perseverance, and patience, you will confidently navigate obstacles, turning challenges into opportunities for growth. Armed with these virtues, you can achieve remarkable things, whether expanding humanity's presence in space or striving for success on Earth. Take that first step today—your journey to greatness begins now.

References

Buglogical Control System. (n.d.). *Ladybugs in space on the shuttle.* https://www.buglogical.com/ladybugs-in-space.

Chopra, R. (Host). (2024, April 10). Women of Power: Host Ritu Chopra speaks with Lumbie Mlambo [Video Podcast]. In *Women of Power.* YouTube. https://www.youtube.com/watch?v=jMWM_miq56o.

Clear, J. (2018). *Atomic habits: An easy & proven way to build good habits & break bad ones.* Penguin Publishing Group.

Dialogo-Americas. (2011, December 20). *Chile Launches its First Space Satellite into Orbit.* Dialogo-Americas.com. https://dialogo-americas.com/articles/chile-launches-its-first-space-satellite-into-orbit/.

Demetri. (2024, March 27). Top 30 Kobe Bryant Quotes About Hard Work & Work Ethic. *Basketball Mindset Training.* https://www.basketballmindsettraining.com/blog/kobe-bryant-hard-work-quotes.

Duckworth, A. (2016). *Grit: The power of passion and perseverance.* Scribner.

Duckworth, A. L. (2013, May 9). *Grit: The Power of Passion and Perseverance* [Video]. YouTube. https://www.youtube.com/watch?v=H14bBuluwB8.

FWM Contributing Authors. (2021, March 23). Lumbie Mlambo, Advocate for Clean Water and Empowering Women Globally. *Formidable Woman Magazine.* https://www.formidablewomanmag.com/lumbie-mlambo-advocate-for-clean-water-and-empowering-women-globally/.

Goodall, J. (n.d.). *Quotable Quote.* Goodreads. Retrieved September 21, 2024, from https://www.goodreads.com/author/quotes/18163.Jane_Goodall?

page=2#:~:text=Without%20patience%20I%20could
%20never%20have%20succeeded.&text=Children
%E2%80%94and%20adults%E2%80%94who
%20have,about%20themselves%20and%20the
%20world.

Pink, D. H. (2011). *Drive: The surprising truth about what motivates us.* Penguin Publishing Group.

Roosevelt, T. (n.d.). *Quotable Quote.* Goodreads. Retrieved September 21, 2024, from https://www.goodreads.com/quotes/7-it-is-not-the-critic-who-counts-not-the-man.

Ryan, M. J. (2021). *The power of patience: How this old-fashioned virtue can improve your life.* Mango Media.

Sam Walton Quotes. (n.d.). BrainyQuote.com. Retrieved September 26, 2024, from https://www.brainyquote.com/quotes/sam_walton_657722.

Shetterly, M. L. (2016). *Hidden figures: The American dream and the untold story of the black women mathematicians who helped win the space race.* HarperCollins.

Sonono, G., & Mlambo, L. (2024, June 12). *Permaculture Association Campfire Events: Individual actions lead to collective impact: 100 voices for our planet* [Video]. YouTube. https://www.youtube.com/watch?v=ICxyTaoGFKE.

Success Podcast. (n.d.). *The Science of Success* [Audio podcast series]. The Science of Success. https://www.successpodcast.com/.

A SPECIAL THANK YOU TO OUR GLOBAL THOUGHT LEADERS

I am deeply grateful to the incredible global thought leaders who generously shared their time, wisdom, and experiences for this book. Their diverse perspectives, drawn from industries spanning aerospace, education, policy, technology, and entrepreneurship, have been invaluable in shaping the lessons presented here. These leaders, who have overcome significant challenges, offer unique insights that enrich each chapter, providing practical examples of resilience, leadership, and innovation.

Through their stories, this book brings to life the principles of success, adaptability, and growth that transcend industries and cultures. Their contributions are not just an inspiration but a roadmap for anyone striving to reach new heights in their personal and professional lives.

Below, you will find brief bios of these remarkable individuals, each a testament to the power of leadership, vision, and the ability to shape the future.

H.E. Dr. Arteaga Serrano, Rosalía

H.E. Dr. Rosalia Arteaga Serrano, an Ecuadorian, is the first woman to serve as President and Vice President of Ecuador. She was Vice Minister of Culture, Minister of Education, Secretary General of the Amazon Cooperation Treaty Organization (OTCA), and a member of the Board of Trustees of the Library of Alexandria and the Editorial Board of the Encyclopedia

Britannica. She is the Executive President of Fundación FIDAL, President of RAW–The Global Women Foundation, and President of UNIR–Ecuador. Dr. Arteaga continues to be a prominent figure in education and international cooperation.

Budholiya, Sejal

Sejal Budholiya is pursuing a master's in strategic product design (Honors) at TU Delft and is a Justus and Louise Van Effen scholarship holder. She holds a bachelor's in mechanical engineering from the Vellore Institute of Technology, where she published four papers, filed four patents, and worked previously at Collins Aerospace. She serves as the Asia Pacific Regional Executive Secretary for the Space Generation Advisory Council and leads the FIGURES team in the Our Giant Leap project group.

She served as the Chairperson of SEDS India and the national representative at SEDS Earth. Sejal is also a published author, a trained artist with a diploma in fine arts, and a Kathak dancer with a senior diploma and degree in folk dance. She co-founded Project Neysa, teaching performing arts to underprivileged children, and is currently researching methods to reduce the gender data gap through design.

Carter, Sandy

Sandy Carter has held distinguished leadership positions as Chief Operations Officer, Chief Marketing Officer, Chief Sales Officer, Channel Chief, and Chief Product Officer at Amazon Web Services (AWS) and International Business Machines Corporation (IBM). Her unique background encompasses a pioneering role in AI innovation, contributing to IBM Watson's development and introducing the first business model for the AI ecosystem. At AWS, Sandy collaborated with C-level customers to address AI needs, leading to innovative solutions. She credits her teams for their success in developing industry-changing AI technologies. Sandy also serves on the Altair Board and has received numerous awards, including AI Executive Champion of the Year and CNN Top 10 Women in Tech.

Chaturvedi, Arpit

Arpit Chaturvedi is the co-founder and CEO of Global Policy Insights and founder/CEO of Insights International. He also founded the GPODS Fellowship and currently serves as an advisor at Teneo. With a master of public administration from Cornell University and an MBA in HR from Symbiosis Centre for Management and Human Resource Development, Arpit is an author and strategic management professional. He is an experienced development consultant skilled in planning, organizational design, HR consulting, systems thinking, and government affairs. Arpit is dedicated to public policy, diplomacy, sustainability, and education, fostering impactful global collaborations across various sectors.

Cohen-Barzilay, Vered Susanne

Vered Cohen-Barzilay is an Israeli-born social entrepreneur and a tenacious aviation, space, and science education advocate. She is the founder and director of "Out of the Box" Social Enterprise, promoting innovation and entrepreneurship in education with a special focus on aerospace. Vered mentors at the United Nations Office for Outer Space Affairs (UNOOSA) Space 4 Women Program, Starburst IAI, and 8200 Impact Accelerators. Recognized by the US Department of State as a #FacesofExchange honoree, she partners with NASA Ames, the US Embassy in Jerusalem, and the Israeli Space Agency. Vered also founded Novel Rights Human Rights Literature and the Women's Media Center Israel, advocating for gender equality and social justice in the media industry.

Del Valle, Michelle

Michelle Del Valle is a young, visionary entrepreneur with a diverse genetic engineering and aerospace technology background. She founded FinSat to enable leaders across corporate, government, and community sectors to develop sustainable urban infrastructure through the Finsat platform that merges satellite data, real-time visualization, and climate adaptation planning.

Before FinSat, Michelle co-founded Stardust, a nonprofit focused on providing technical skills in aerospace to at-risk youth. Her career also includes significant roles in Fortune 500 pharmaceuticals (Regeneron), the Space Frontier Foundation's NewSpace Conference, and a diverse real estate portfolio across the US. She has contributed to various initiatives, including those at the National Institute on Minority Health and Health Disparities and Howard Hughes Medical Institute. Michelle is a graduate of the University of Texas.

Dipert, Adam, PhD

Adam Dipert has worked as a nuclear physics researcher at NC State, Duke, and Los Alamos National Lab. His career as a professional circus performer stimulated a passion for exploring the intriguing connections between movement and mathematics and finding innovative ways to share these interdisciplinary links with others. Through this combination of scientific and artistic exploration, he brings a unique perspective to teach and inspire a deeper understanding of physical and mathematical concepts.

Dr. Farsadaki, Vanessa

Dr. Vanessa Farsadaki is a visionary leader in space health with over six years of experience. She is the President and managing partner of Space Exploration Strategies, where she oversees cutting-edge space health programs to enhance astronaut safety and well-being. Vanessa, along with an MD, also holds a BSc in biology, an MSc in genetics, an MS in astrophysics, an MBA, and an EMGM in space leadership and leverages her expertise to provide strategic advice across various sectors. A certified NSS space ambassador and BIS fellow, she is an international keynote speaker and author of multiple publications on space health. Vanessa excels in research, project management, communication, and leadership.

Goddard, Gabriella

Gabriella Goddard is the founder of Brainsparker, an award-winning business that has ignited the creativity of over half a million people across the globe. With innovative training programs, card decks, coaching kits, and a top-ranked creativity app, Brainsparker has transformed lives worldwide. In 2023, Gabriella won Greater London's Businesswoman of the Year and the Globee® Silver Award for Women in Business (Micro-Business). As an innovation catalyst, she has over 20 years of experience coaching leaders to innovate and build high-performing teams. She is an alumna of the International Space University and serves as a mentor for the UK Space Agency Accelerator and UNOOSA's Space4Women program. She is the top-selling author of *Gulp!* and contributes articles to Forbes as a member of the Forbes Coaches Council.

Gozen, Machiko

Machiko Gozen, CEO of GOZEN Tech Ltd, champions women's empowerment and innovation, infusing happiness by connecting minds to sustainably transformative projects. Raised in a samurai woman's family in Kanazawa, Japan, she translates the wisdom of bushido into sustainable solutions using advanced technologies.

Machiko leads initiatives supporting women in tech and wellness, promoting the spirit of "wabi-sabi"—finding beauty in imperfection. Notably, she led the creation of the Guinness record-winning 5.8-meter-diameter rose origami. As president of Vendôme Tea Group, she oversees one of the largest organic green tea plantations, dedicated to mindfulness and community empowerment through tea. Machiko aims to collaborate with visionary leaders to create a better tomorrow.

Haldeman, Ben

Ben Haldeman founded LifeShip, a community space movement that preserves copies of Earth in space. With LifeShip, anyone can send their DNA, stories, dreams, art, and more to the Moon and beyond. Ben possesses a rocket science mind grounded in a human journey of exploration and expansion. Ben is an investor and advisor to several space companies. He was an early engineer at Planet Lab, designing spacecraft to record our changing planet. He built telescopes to find new exoplanets and created instruments to look for life on Mars. Ben lives in San Diego with his daughter, Luna.

Johnson, Karlton D.

Karlton Johnson is the Chief Executive Officer and Chairman of the Board at the National Space Society and the CEO of DeLaine Strategy Group LLC. He leads a premier strategic advisory firm renowned for guiding Fortune 500 companies and innovative sectors in the commercial and civil space. DeLaine Strategy Group specializes in transforming complex challenges into strategic opportunities and driving sustainable growth through cybersecurity, space development, and strategic risk management. Karlton's mission is to forge deep partnerships with C-suite leaders, co-creating the future of global industries and empowering executives to lead tomorrow's innovations with confidence and resilience.

Joy, Iroka Chidinma, PhD

Iroka Chidinma Joy is an Assistant Director and Head of the Satellite and Navigation Systems in the Engineering and Space System Department of Nigeria's National Space Research and Development Agency (NASRDA). She was the only woman on the RF team that designed, built, and tested the Nigerian satellites NigSat-2 and NigSat-X.

Her master's thesis focused on rain attenuation at Ka-Band, and she led the PalmSat-Nig S-Band Microwave Beacon project. Iroka holds a PhD in communication engineering and is a UNOOSA Space Ambassador, African Space Leadership Congress Women Leader, and co-founder of Women in Aerospace Nigeria. She is passionate about promoting STEM among women and girls in Africa.

Kim, KangSan (Antonio Stark)

KangSan Kim (Antonio Stark) is a space policy, strategy, and cooperation expert from South Korea. He currently works as the Global Alliance Lead at Ispace, Inc., a multinational lunar transportation and resource development company. Over his 10 years in the space sector, Antonio has worked with multiple space agencies in the region, and his research expertise covers cislunar exploration, human spaceflight, material sciences, and the application of AI tools for space.

Antonio is a member of multiple NGOs, including the Space Generation Advisory Council, Moon Village Association, and the Space Court Foundation. He is an International Astronautical Federation Emerging Space Leader and a recipient of the ISDC Excellence Award by the National Space Society.

Lupushor, Stela

Stela Lupushor is dedicated to humanizing the workplace through innovation, execution, education, and thought leadership. She collaborates with startups and venture funds to develop products and investment strategies that enhance workplace experiences. As a consultant at Reframe.Work, Inc., she advises organizational leaders on creating exceptional workplace environments using technology and human-centered design. Stela also teaches Digital Workplace Design and Design Thinking at NYU. She co-founded the Strategic HR Analytics Meet-up, co-authored books on optimizing business returns through people, and holds a patent pending for a social sentiment analysis tool. Stela is a recognized speaker on People Analytics and the Future of Work.

Mlambo, Lumbie

Lumbie Mlambo, featured on the 2024 Women to Watch List, is an impact entrepreneur passionate about women's issues. She founded JB Dondolo, a nonprofit that provides clean water, sanitation, and hygiene to underserved communities, focusing on women and girls. Lumbie created the *100 Voices for Our Planet* initiative to inspire eco-conscious living and amplify voices advocating for sustainability. A UN Global Leadership Award recipient and Global Goals Ambassador, she has been recognized with numerous accolades, including the AWIEF Social Entrepreneur Award and the Nasdaq Milestone Maker. Lumbie serves as a mentor and advisor, championing clean water (SDG 6) and gender equality (SDG 5), working tirelessly to ensure equitable access to opportunities for all.

Morrow, Monique

With over 25 years of experience, Monique Morrow is a global technology leader known for driving business growth and innovation. She is a venture partner at Sparklabs Accelerator for Cybersecurity and Blockchain and an independent director on the Hedera Hashgraph Board. Previously, she was a senior distinguished architect for emerging technologies at Syniverse Technologies. Monique is President and co-founder of the Humanized Internet, focusing on digital identity and ethics. Recognized by Forbes and Cybersecurity Ventures, she holds over 17 patents and has co-authored several books. Monique has an MSc in digital currency and blockchain, an MS in telecommunications, an MBA, and is a doctoral student in cyberpsychology.

Naseem, Mariam

Mariam Naseem is a multifaceted professional passionate about the convergence of emerging technologies and space exploration. She researches icy ocean worlds as a PhD student in planetary geology at the University of Maryland, College Park. With engineering experience on a Russian oil rig and a product development center in Texas, she honed her skills in field operations and production planning. Mariam has also worked as a commercial space consultant, strategist, and business development manager in deep tech. A visiting scholar at the Blue Marble Space Institute of Science, she champions diversity and encourages women and underrepresented minorities to pursue careers in space.

Nowajewski-Barra, Priscilla, PhD

Priscilla Nowajewski is an astronomer and climatologist

working as a data analyst at the Atacama Large Millimeter/ Submillimeter Array (ALMA) in northern Chile, the world's most advanced astronomical observatory. With a PhD in fluid dynamics specializing in planetary atmospheres, Priscilla investigates the atmospheric dynamics present at the Chilean altiplano, the atmospheric conditions for life on other planets, and the impact of the global dust storms on Mars's surface. She is the first Chilean woman to publish on planetary atmospheres and habitability and co-founded Chile's first Planetary Sciences Foundation. Leading the Chilean chapter of the Mars Society, she inspires young scientists. At ALMA, she developed an in-house weather forecast system and automated calibration processes, enhancing operational efficiency. Priscilla embodies perseverance, curiosity, and scientific excellence.

Pereira, Linda, PhD

Linda Pereira is the G100 Global Chair for Communication & Advocacy, a university lecturer, CNN commentator, entrepreneur, and top meeting & event planner. As a message architect and stage presenter, she has won numerous awards, including the Business Spirit Award and the 2008 Business Owner Award. Recognized among the top 100 women in eCommerce and recipient of the IAHMP Education Award, Linda mentors at three universities and serves on multiple boards. She is the President of APPEN and an advisory board member of Meetings Show UK. In 2013, she won the WE Magazine USA award for Global Marketing.

Prazakova, Andrea

Andrea Prazakova is a human-centered AI expert with 32 years of experience in banking, tech, and payments; bringing a global perspective from her work across Europe, Asia, Africa, and the Middle East. Andrea has led groundbreaking projects with a proven track record in transforming industries, from setting up retail and small and medium enterprise (SME) banks across Africa to pioneering customer experience initiatives in Europe. Her commitment to creating technology that prioritizes people and the planet is evident in her co-founding of *Space Uncensored*, a podcast dedicated to elevating women's roles in the space and AI economy. Armed with MIT, INSEAD, and Stanford certifications, Andrea is a relentless advocate for AI strategies that ensure human longevity and ecological balance. She is also an investor, public speaker, and the founder of AndreaNow and BrainGym.

Sadou, Asta-Adji

Asta-Adji Sadou is the founder of Scoops Mak, a Fulani Cooperative Society for Sustainable Development, a community leader, and a mechanical engineer. She is a dedicated science communicator, climate change advocate, and female gender-based activist with expertise in project management, energy-efficient systems, precision agriculture, sustainability, and green technologies.

She is passionate about making science and engineering accessible to all, especially women from marginalized communities. She is committed to designing innovative solutions that reduce environmental impact. Combining technical skills with a deep understanding of ecological challenges, Asta actively engages in projects promoting sustainable practices, aiming to contribute to a greener and more resilient future. She also works to bridge the gap between complex scientific concepts and the general public.

Her advocacy for gender equality focuses on amplifying the voices of women and girls in science, thereby addressing gender-based violence. Through her work, Asta-Adji Sadou aims to empower women, promote inclusive education, and strive to create sustainable engineering solutions that address the urgent needs of our planet while fostering a more equitable society for all.

Samanga, Ruvimbo

Ruvimbo Samanga is a Space Law & Policy Analyst and Researcher dedicated to capacity building in the African and global space sector. She is passionate about the intersection of space with trade, investment, human rights, and social sciences, so she actively seeks collaboration for space-related research. As a Milo Space Science Institute Ambassador at Arizona State University and a board member at the Space Arbitration Association, Ruvimbo integrates her deep appreciation for the creative arts into her work, inspiring education, business, and leadership. Committed to community engagement, she values meaningful relationships and strives to inspire others through her journey in the space industry.

Spitz, Roger

Roger Spitz (BSc in Econ, MSc, FCA, APF) is a bestselling author and world-leading authority on strategic foresight and systems innovations. As President of Techistential and Chair of the Disruptive Futures Institute, he advises CEOs and boards on strategy under uncertainty. Roger has given keynotes globally, lectured at top institutions, and published widely on anticipatory leadership and futures intelligence.

His book, *Disrupt With Impact*, and his acclaimed collection, *The Definitive Guide to Thriving on Disruption*, have been adopted worldwide. An expert in climate foresight and AI, he founded the Techistential Center for Human & Artificial Intelligence and serves on multiple boards, including Lux Carbon Standard. Roger is on the non-profit Teach the Future board, which offers futures thinking education programs for young students globally.

Talebi, Bryan

Bryan Talebi began his career as an aerospace engineer at NASA when he was 16 years old. In college, he built a business selling educational products, reaching $1M in annual revenue before starting and selling a consulting company. He then joined ZocDoc as a manager, helping scale it to unicorn status. Bryan is the CEO & co-founder of Ahura AI, which enables accelerated learning and targets workforce development for those displaced by technological unemployment. He is also the chairman of Neural Tunes, which uses AI and music to heal PTSD, depression, and anxiety, and co-founded AB+ Ventures.

Trabinski, Piotr

Piotr Trabinski has a multidisciplinary background with double master's degrees in law and computer science/cybersecurity and over 15 years of experience in macroeconomic policy analysis, financial sector supervision, and digital transformation. His expertise includes fiscal, monetary, and financial sector policies, as well as digital currencies and Web3. Piotr has led high-impact policy engagements with the International Monetary Fund (IMF), the World Bank, and the US Department of State, providing economic rationale for increased infrastructure investment in Central and Eastern Europe. He has advised on a post-war Ukraine recovery strategy and delivered institutional reform proposals to ten governments. Piotr excels in team leadership, stakeholder relations, and operational excellence.

Von Storch, Klaus

Klaus Von Storch is a distinguished IT strategist and aerospace engineer. A former lieutenant colonel and fighter pilot in the Chilean Air Force, he also trained on Mirage Cheetah aircraft in South Africa. Klaus holds a bachelor's of science in aerospace engineering from the University of Southern California and has worked with the Chilean Space Agency since 1993. Selected for Space Shuttle training in 2000 and later as a candidate for a Russian spacecraft mission to the ISS, he remains an active cosmonaut candidate. Klaus is a pilot for SKY Airline and excels in clean energy projects, digital transformation, and regulatory compliance.

Wang, Ke

Ke is the founding partner of Timenschen Fund, where she initiated the fund for cross-border investment and local capabilities development in the space industry in the Middle East and Northern African (MENA) region. Ke is also the founder of Timenschen Institute. The Institute's purpose is to connect the MENA region and other space-faring nations through R&D,

education, and cultural exchange. At Disrupt Space, Ke inspires and engages people from diverse backgrounds to create and grow new space ventures. She organizes summits and provides market entry services, supply chain integration, and financial advisory services.

In 2019, she co-founded the Karman Project Foundation to foster global collaboration in the space sector. Ke's initiatives include the Karman Week and Gala Dinner, the Karman Impact Fund, and strategic partnerships with key organizations. She holds a master's in management from the *École Supérieure de Commerce de Paris* (ESCP) Business School and is an Oxford Fellow in space commerce and governance.

Wysenyuy, Desmond Fonyuy

Desmond Fonyuy Wysenyuy is a space engineer and geospatial expert with over 10 years of experience in satellite communication, project management, and corporate strategy. He has worked with the United Nations, Arizona State University, SERVIR West Africa (NASA and USAID), and Digital Earth (DE) Africa. He holds master's degrees in global management from Thunderbird School of Global Management and in space science and technology. Desmond has lectured at the UN-African Regional Institute and trained Nigerian law enforcement in geospatial techniques. He founded SpaceGate Way, a nonprofit dedicated to space education and training young African professionals.

Yazici, Tuana

Tuana Yazici is the founder, chair, and CEO of Tuana Group, AeroAI Voyages, AeroAI DesignLab, and the nonprofit AeroAI Global Solutions. These entities collectively aim to leverage AI and space technologies to improve global living conditions.

As a third-year law student and member of the International Institute of Space Law, Yazici holds a master's in international administration with a concentration in space policy and a BA in philosophy, politics, and economics (PPE) with a minor in psychology, having completed both degrees a year early. With recent publications in space law and policy, Yazici is a featured speaker at global conferences, sharing insights into her work. She has also written and illustrated four children's books, donating all profits to various charities.

Aside from work, Yazici is a student helicopter pilot working towards a private license. In her free time, Yazici enjoys painting, doing martial arts, playing the piano, skiing, wakeboarding, windsurfing, and flyboarding.

ABOUT THE AUTHOR

Shelli Brunswick

Shelli Brunswick is a distinguished space innovation leader known for her visionary perspective and profound influence on the global space community.

Her remarkable journey began with a distinguished career in the US Air Force, where she excelled in space acquisition, program management, and congressional liaison roles. Transitioning seamlessly to her role as Chief Operating Officer of Space Foundation and now as the CEO & Founder of SB Global LLC, Shelli's leadership is defined by strategic engagement and advocacy that shape the global space ecosystem.

A passionate advocate for space technology and access, Shelli's collaborations span commercial, governmental, and educational sectors worldwide, reflecting her commitment to fostering a progressive and inclusive space landscape.

As a prolific author and sought-after keynote speaker, Shelli delivers motivational speeches, inspiring global audiences on career success, leadership, and innovation. Her thought leadership is evident in her publications in SpaceNews, Forbes Technology Council, and her involvement with esteemed think tanks like the Hudson Institute and the Wilson Center.

Shelli's influence extends beyond the present, contributing to NASA and European Space Agency research initiatives and shaping the future of global space exploration. Her dedication to women in space has earned her numerous accolades, including two Lifetime Achievement Awards, Top 100 Women of the

Future in Emerging Technology, and the Chief in Tech Award. She was included in the 100 Voices for Our Planet, an initiative of the United Nations Environment Programme (UNEP) that recognizes individuals for their contributions to sustainability and global environmental challenges.

Her leadership extends to key roles such as Chair of the Tod'Aérs Global Network and the Global Council for the Promotion of International Trade (GCPIT) Global Alliance for Space Economy. She also serves as Board Chair for Manufacturer's Edge, a strategic partner for the US Department of Commerce, and a board member for AeroAI Global Solutions and the Global Women Leaders Committee of the World Business Angels Investment Forum.

. To reach the author, please send an email to whatsspacegottodowithit@gmail.com.

Please join the conversation at
https://shelli-brunswick.com